MW01505584

"Might be the most important book in Young Life in the last twenty-five years."

— Brent Cunningham, Area Developer, rural Alaska

"Eric Protzman combines the passion of an evangelist and the pragmatism of an engineer. You'll see the vulnerability of a follower of Christ as he unpacks his journey with Andy and reaches adolescents with the message of God's love. Joy, frustration, and humility are raw and relatable in this book. Through fresh eyes we accept once again that it takes a community to reach a community. When it happens, everyone is changed!"

— Ken Tankersley, SVP Young Life Community Networks

"This book is a human story of relationships, communities, and changes. It offers a prime opportunity to gain insights that apply to all relationships and communities we serve."

— Claudia Mitchell

"These two formed one of the most effective partnerships I have seen in my thirty years in the mission of Young Life."

— Terry Leprino, Regional Director, Front Range Region

"For seventeen years, I have had an Area Director come home to me at the end of the day, and I can attest to the high highs and the low lows of ministry. *Our Town, Our Kids* tells a true story about how Young Life can not only be a gift to kids in our town but how it can be a blessing to those called to it."

— Genna Morman, wife of Andy Morman

"A fresh and vulnerable book about doing ministry right. Here's the question: How can the Holy Spirit grab hold of a rapidly deteriorating ministry relationship between two seasoned Christians and transform it into something very special, even enviable? *Our Town, Our Kids* reminds us that the gospel can do it."

— Dr. Bill Senyard, Gospel App Ministries and author of *Fair Forgiveness: Finding the Power to Forgive Where You Least Expect It*

"I've heard Eric and Andy tell this story dozens of times and I believe in it more now than ever. I have seen Young Life Areas and ultimately people transformed because of the vulnerability of Eric and Andy's journey together. For all the mistakes shared honestly in these pages, God has faithfully redeemed every single one."

— Kimberly Silvernale, Divisional Operations Manager, Young Life Northwest Division

"When Committee Chairs and Area Directors model true spiritual friendship the results can be miraculous. *Our Town, Our Kids* reflects Jesus' loving instruction to send them out two by two."

— Gill Richard, Regional Board Chairman,
Front Range Region

"When I replaced Andy Morman as Area Director, I walked into the fruit of this book. I too discovered when I am in true partnership with my Committee Chair, I don't survive, I thrive. My heart is keenly drawn to women and moms on staff. There is a path in this book for women on staff to thrive."

— Kaylan Riley, Area Director Intermountain Young Life

"In *Our Town, Our Kids*, Eric thoughtfully reflects on his years as a Young Life Committee Chair. In doing so, he provides a roadmap for all of those who are following in his footsteps. It is a must read for Young Life Staff and Committee Chairs."

— Jacque Abadie, Regional Director, Front Range Region

"An honest and open reflection of a well-intended relationship between an Area Director and Committee Chair that left a lot of hurt and pain. As a Regional Director I have seen this unnecessary spiral happen too many times. We can and must do better. *Our Town, Our Kids* is a must read for any Young Life community."

— TJ Dickerson, Regional Director Rocky Mountain Region

"A must read for every Young Life Area! I watched Eric and Andy's story in its pain and beautiful redemption. The reimagined Area Director and Committee Chair relationship is transformative. Ask the questions in the book. Enjoy the journey!

— Jeb Baum, former IMYL Committee Chair,
YL Volunteer Leader, grateful YL dad

"Committee Chairs will learn so much here. This raw account shows how God can make all things new. Eric and Andy share hard-earned wisdom for every YL Area! Using their approach, the transition to serving Intermountain Young Life was seamless. Eric continues to serve as a friend, coach, and encouragement to me and to Intermountain Young Life."

— Krista Wallace, three-time Committee Chair,
domestic and international,
and current Committee Chair, Intermountain Young Life

"I had the privilege of working with Andy as Committee Chair after he and Eric discovered this new model of true partnership in Young Life ministry. It was a model Andy and I committed to, and I'm grateful that Eric lays out the lessons and practices so clearly. A game-changer for your Area Director and Committee Chair relationship.

— Taylor Wolfe, Committee Chair, Issaquah, WA

"I sat next to Eric over the years as this unfolded. The story of Eric and Andy is accurate and at times painful. It offers great hope for ministries seeking to fulfill their mission."

— Howard Hargrove, Rocky Mountain Regional Field Missionary for Fathers in the Field

"Our Town, Our Kids opens up the underbelly of ministry with flawed people and reveals the beauty of living out solid biblical principles. The goal is kids knowing Jesus and it really matters! *Our Town, Our Kids*...OURS! Thank you, Eric."

— Cindy Yohann, Committee Developer

"Pastors, please read this book. Accessible and memorable. Share it with a fellow pastor, especially someone wanting to deepen their relationships while not abandoning their organizational goals. The leadership and relationship principles very much apply to church ministry."

— Jason Freeman, lead pastor, Bergen Park Church, Evergreen, CO

OUR TOWN, OUR KIDS

REIMAGINING YOUR YOUNG LIFE AREA

ERIC PROTZMAN

ILLUMIFY
MEDIA.COM

Our Town, Our Kids

Copyright © 2023 by Eric Protzman

Published by
Illumify Media Global
www.IllumifyMedia.com
"Let's bring your book to life!"

Paperback ISBN: 978-1-959099-28-4

Typeset by Jennifer Clark
Cover design by Debbie Lewis

Printed in the United States of America

CONTENTS

GLOSSARY OF TERMS

Christ (Savior and Lord)
Area Director (AD)
Campaigners (weekly Bible-based study with Leaders,
also known as Groups)
Club (weekly party with a purpose for kids to gather
with Leaders)
Committee Chair (CC)
Committee members (YL Committee)
Community (our IMYL towns)
Intermountain Young Life (IMYL, our YL Area, CO37)
Kids (adolescents/students)
Leaders (in direct ministry with our kids; often called
Volunteer Leaders)
Staff (or Young Life Staff, paid YL Staff)
Volunteers/Donors (supporters joining a story)
Young Life (or YL, founded 1941)

FOREWORD

When Eric told me he wanted to write a book about our story, the news was both exciting and sobering. After all, the story Eric and I lived and the lessons we learned mark one of the hardest seasons of my life.

When I started my new role as Area Director of Intermountain Young Life in 2008, I was brimming with excitement and confidence. Eric, as Committee Chairman, was my biggest fan, placing his full trust in me.

Unfortunately, a fatal flaw in the roles we had defined for ourselves created a ticking time bomb, and when things went south, it was devastating. I felt lonely and isolated. Sometimes I felt attacked and blamed.

Fearing I was about to be fired, some days I couldn't get myself out of bed. My wife and kids experienced the fallout of what I thought was going to be the end of my time on Staff. I felt defeated and estranged from the man who had been my biggest fan.

Area Directors, Committee members, paid Staff members, or Volunteers can get discouraged. You may have experienced some of the same frustrations and obstacles that played a role in our story.

Eric and I often share our story in the Young Life community. Many people have experienced our kind of pain, isolation, tension, and mismanaged expectations. We experienced so much of this before God intervened.

One evening, while my wife was putting our children to bed, I felt wound up. While mopping the kitchen floor in our apartment, my mind was spinning with hypothetical conversations I wanted to have with Eric. These imaginary conversations were dripping with accusations and self-defense.

All of a sudden, I realized this is not the way it is supposed to be.

"God," I prayed aloud, "will you help me? I am tired and can't handle this anymore."

Then I did something which five minutes earlier I couldn't have done. I called Eric and said, "I'm sorry."

Eric said, "I'm sorry too."

Then God did a miracle. Immediately, He began to mend our broken hearts. He revealed to us what we had been doing wrong. He showed us that too many other Area Directors and Committees were drowning in the same currents.

Eric and I were both called to this work, and it was now threatened. We had undermined our relationship. In this miracle, He began to mend our broken hearts.

Today, Eric and I are the best of friends. He is someone I trust fully and can rely on in ministry and life.

This story of restoration has been one of the most incredible miracles in my life.

Eric and I went from a frustrating leader-helper model to a true partnership. We experienced courage, equality, and freedom. This resulted in a deeper impact on the youth in our community.

How we got here—and the lessons we learned along the way—are a powerful testimony to God's redemptive powers. His desire is to grow all of us into the people and ministers he wants us to be. We believe the hard road we traveled is avoidable.

There is a better way. We lived it, and you can too.

—Andy Morman

INTRODUCTION

*Children are a heritage from the L*ORD*, offspring a reward from him.*

—Psalm 127:3

For when we came into Macedonia, we had no rest, but we were harassed at every turn—conflicts on the outside, fears within.

—2 Corinthians 7:5

We made so many mistakes in the Intermountain Young Life Area.

As Committee Chair (CC), I took on too little responsibility and learned hard lessons.

As Area Director (AD), Andy Morman took on too much responsibility and learned hard lessons.

We created misunderstandings bigger than either of us. As a result, we suffered a severe falling out which lasted years. It breaks our hearts to know, if left up to us, we wouldn't be speaking today.

Thankfully, the Holy Spirit showed us we weren't

expecting too much of each other—we were expecting too little.

He showed us how to begin carrying each other's burdens.

People you know may be walking our same destructive path. In sharing our story and hard-won lessons, I hope your community and kids will prosper. Staff lonesomeness went away and Volunteer engagement increased in our reimagined Area.

The tangle of Area leadership was at the heart of our struggle, and it's at the heart of this book.

Here's a bit of my story.

Most kids whose lives change through Young Life, or YL, remember their Leader's name, but I didn't. Thirty-seven long years after meeting Jesus at a YL Club at Omaha Benson High School, I attended a YL Leadership Weekend at Crooked Creek Ranch in Colorado. I was on a work crew serving food to a new generation of overcommitted Leaders. I happened to be wearing a Nebraska T-shirt I'd snagged from my duffel. A guy next to me waiting to fill his tray pointed to my shirt. He said years ago he'd tried to start a YL Club in Nebraska. We explored some connections and figured the whole thing out.

He was the Young Life Leader who led me to Christ.

Paul Petersen and I dragged a couple of chairs off to a quiet corner and released decades of tears.

For six weeks in 1971, Paul had busted up Interstate 80 from Lincoln for over an hour to Omaha Benson High School. This was always after a day of his own classes at the University of Nebraska. He tried to get a Club started. It didn't take. He'd taken on too much.

His commitment became unsustainable. The result was unimaginable.

He left the attempt dejected. "I never thought I did any good at all," Paul told me through tears.

In truth he *had* done life-altering good. He had entered my life and changed it forever, but his exhaustion and lonesomeness had taken its toll.

We need to understand why we have so many lonesome Staff, Volunteers and even Committee members who feel the isolating weight of ministry.

I've experienced walking in Paul's lonesome shoes. So has Andy. As have dedicated YL Leaders, Staff, and Volunteers around the world. There is a healthier, less heroic option.

Andy and I pray for your joy and success.

Andy Morman and Eric Protzman 2017

ARE YOU SETTING YOURSELF UP FOR DISAPPOINTMENT IN THE FIRST TEN MINUTES?

Consider it pure joy, my brothers, and sisters, whenever you face trials of many kinds, because you know that the testing of your faith produces perseverance. Let perseverance finish its work so that you may be mature and complete, not lacking anything.

— James 1:2–4

"I'm going to close down Club for the next nine months for a reset." Andy, our Young Life Area Director, shocked me with his statement.

We were in Andy's office, sitting on opposite sides of his desk. His words made me furious.

"The problem is low-energy, uninspiring Clubs," I pushed back. "Our Young Life ministry is too small, and I don't think you are up to the job. The way to fix uninspiring Clubs is to practice making inspiring Clubs—not quit for nine months."

Andy did not hesitate. "Young Life is the expert in kid ministry, and you need to stay out of it. Your input is not welcome."

This stomped on a nerve.

"If you are such experts, why is it failing?" I asked him. "I'm withdrawing all my support, financial and otherwise."

This shameful confrontation occurred in 2011, just three years after our community had hired Andy to lead Intermountain Young Life.

How did we get to this godless moment?

WE STARTED WITH THE BEST INTENTIONS.

Back in 2007, a gap divided our town and our kids. Adults often saw middle and high school kids as thoughtful and fantastic. We also saw them as confusing and intimidating. Inspiring students in our town to learn about Jesus left us feeling inadequate.

My wife, Nancy, and I saw the gap and were looking for our role in youth ministry. For more than nine months we canvassed our community. We engaged with pastors, youth pastors, coaches, and teachers. We looked for anybody, spiritual or secular, who loved teenagers. We wanted to learn about those who preceded us in ministry in our town. Supporting them was our priority.

"Go meet Ben and Judy McComb," Pastor Philip Reimers advised us. "They have been at the center of youth ministry for decades. They have a Young Life background."

I was well aware of the impact of the organization. Nancy and I had had a long relationship as Committee members with Young Life before we moved to the mountains.

"We've been waiting for you," Ben told us when we met.

Ben and Judy have had a long history of humble, obedient ministry. Their primary focus has always been serving disinterested kids. These kids are sometimes forgotten in the shuffle. Visible, involved kids are the focus of most sacred and secular organizations. Disinterested kids are those who don't have a connection with faith in their family or circle of friends.

They rarely hear the gospel straight. In 2007, these kids hadn't been much of a focus in our town. Thankfully, they are the specialty of Young Life. In fact, Young Life has stood in this gap since 1941.

Ben and Judy said Evergreen had been without YL for twenty years. Soon five couples formed a Committee and relaunched Intermountain Young Life. We wanted to serve disinterested kids in Evergreen and Idaho Springs, Colorado.

Clueless, we messed up in the first ten minutes.

Our first job was to hire an Area Director.

This new Committee interviewed Andy Morman in the comfort of our living room. Andy and his wife, Genna, arrived with smiles and potential. Andy was carrying his future and ours. We warmed to each other right away. It was a thrilling moment.

Andy is the kind of person you'd want in your town working with your kids. He loves kids, and he loves Jesus. On that first night of our interview, Andy and Genna arrived steered by faith and filled with hope. They brought with them one-year-old Grace. Today Grace is in her teens and is a beautiful, gifted young woman with two younger siblings. She giggled and rolled around under the coffee table. We chatted with her parents, and it all felt like progress.

Andy was anxious to tackle his leadership role and prove he was up to it. He projected an energetic *I've got this covered* posture. This wasn't out of the ordinary, as Young Life Area Directors are trained to lead.

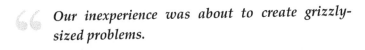

> **Our inexperience was about to create grizzly-sized problems.**

In other words, Andy would provide all the direction, and we would *help*. Figuratively, he tore open his shirt and displayed Superman's red *S*.

This was a relief to us. We wanted an expert who could

shepherd our town while we cheered him on. In return, we promised to bake cookies, raise money, and fund salaries and expenses.

We prayed a grateful prayer, decided Andy was ideal, and polished off dessert.

We had chosen the right person but made a crucial error. This error would limit our impact. Our inexperience was about to create grizzly-sized problems. We didn't have a clue what was heading our way.

OUR SUCCESS WAS UNSUSTAINABLE.

Our community supported the reconstituted YL Area with prayer. The Committee and Volunteers encouraged Staff members. They showed up at events and meetings and wolfed Nancy's famous chocolate chip cookies. We raised money. We waited for Andy and Young Life to produce results. And they did.

Club grew to as many as eighty-five students. Andy found kids, Andy found leaders, kids found hope . . . and kids found Jesus. Our first summer camp trip to Castaway in Minnesota was a triumph. There was so much good happening. Our town was grateful.

As promised, Andy was in charge. He was our leader. He involved himself in fund-raising, community events, and Leader dinners. We called ourselves *partners* with Andy and Young Life. We were more like fans, cheerleaders. We were helpers.

Nobody could have guessed the mistake we made in our first meeting was about to make itself known.

So, what was the error we had made in the first ten minutes?

We had not adopted enough responsibility.

Three years into the experience there was trouble in paradise. The Area seemed to be losing momentum.

I remember a pivotal conversation with Jeb Baum, our second Committee Chair. If you can trust anybody in this world for wisdom, grace, and discernment, it's Jeb. Sitting in the living room where we had hired Andy, I poured two cups of coffee—before saying aloud the next words I paused for some time. "I have a feeling this ministry is becoming unhealthy," I confided. "We've done good things, but we're losing altitude."

"How so?"

"I don't feel we've got the momentum we had in 2008." I cleared my throat. "We may need to replace Andy."

Jeb shook his head. "What? No. Everyone loves Andy, and he's doing a great job. If there are problems, we should go back to the basics and figure out how to do the whole project better."

Young Life started in Dallas in 1941. As it grew, it developed a hierarchical organization to cope with disbursed operations. This was an accepted and useful organizational style for its time. As YL moved beyond Dallas, the top-down structure continued to be used. Young Life Staff were the dispatched experts on whose shoulders success or failure rested. Local helpers were recruited. Committees were conceived for financing this geographic expansion.

The Committee Chair Handbook says, "Decision making is one of the most misunderstood concepts in Young Life, and as a Committee Chair it will be necessary for you to understand and manage decision making along with the Area Director and Regional Director."[1]

Also in the handbook is the following section: "Characteristic #5: Effective Committees Understand Authority and Decision Making in Young Life."

This section of the handbook defines Area Director and Committee roles: "The Area Director and Committee should develop a relationship that values trust and collaboration. At the local level, the Area Director and the Committee should be involved in long-range, major decision making. Committee input and ownership of important decisions are critical."

Then specifically it says, "Committee members should not become involved in the day-to-day operational decisions that are regulated to Young Life Staff."

To clarify decision making, both the Committee Handbook and the Committee Chair Handbook stress that "Young Life Committees are advisory in nature and have no formal authority."[2] Based on these directives, many experienced Young Life Volunteers conclude that the community supports YL, and YL saves our kids.

Why detail this? In the work Andy and I have done with Committees around the country, we generally observe the following issues:

- underutilization of Committees
- overloading of Area Directors
- Areas undershooting their potential reach
- lonesome Staff

Based on our experience the onus is not sufficiently shared. Staff need broader support, and our town seeks ministry with maximum reach.

As a result of the strong Area Director and limited Committee roles, our town can think of Young Life as a turnkey operation that simply needs local help and support. Of course, Young Life does not say turnkey. Young Life does not believe it is turnkey. But a Committee or community might see it this way.

I know because this was the mind-set of IMYL as our town began this journey with YL.

While a partnership is formally requested and described, the leader-helper model undermines it. And while ADs embrace being in charge, they can find the experience isn't as advertised. The leader-helper format imposes isolation on the AD. As helpers lose steam, isolation gets worse.

Insufficient organizational support for youth ministers is epidemic in the church and in other youth ministry. Unreasonable expectations are often placed on dedicated but vulnerable youth ministers. The result? A disenchanted young minister in a struggling, isolated ministry. All towns need healthy ministries who need healthy ministers. We must do all we can to bring all available resources to this goal.

We did find a way out!

But in the meantime . . .

Andy got lonesome.

Then Andy got blamed. By me.

Our IMYL Club succeeded for three years. Then we declined to near failure. As a helper, I blamed our leader, Andy, when ministry declined. I did not realize how much of the problem was me and the expectations of our town.

As we get further into explaining the process, you'll see how I failed.

But ultimately, together we did not succumb. We serve a kind King.

We spent six years solving the problems we had manufactured in the first ten minutes. Through the process I describe in this book, we experienced a new movement of God's love for our town and our kids. This happened when we found solutions to Staff lonesomeness and helper frustration

Intermountain Young Life started with lofty intentions. How did we get this so wrong? How did we end up with lonesomeness and an impaired ministry? Was the root of the problem unrealistic assumptions and expectations?

No, the root of the problem was way worse.

Let me tell you why.

2

ARE YOU OUTSOURCING YOUR KIDS' SALVATION?

As for parents . . . raise them with discipline and instruction about the Lord.

—*Ephesians 6:4 CEB*

"How do you view your personal responsibility for your town and your kids and their salvation?"

I was addressing a dozen men and women sitting in the living room of a southern Colorado Committee Chair. Each of us was serving on Area Committees around the state.

I knew my question was provocative. And, sure enough, I got a prickly response.

"What are you talking about?" someone asked.

I rephrased my question. "Are there responsibilities designated to our Area Directors which belong to our town? Have we outsourced our kids' salvation? [1]

"We love and care for our kids," someone—I'll call him Jeff —answered. "We take responsibility. After all, we brought Young Life into our town."

Others in the room nodded in agreement.

I understand Jeff's perspective. It's the perspective of many Committee members and Committee Chairs. Indeed, it was *my* perspective for many years.

We want our students to hear the gospel. We haven't been as spiritually successful within our town as we'd like. There are many disinterested kids who are generations removed from family faith. We haven't communicated the good news well enough to our own children. It's easy to presume someone else must be able to do it better.

But here's the danger: a community can be looking for the cavalry to come riding over the hill to save our kids.

Look, on the galloping horse! It's our new Area Director!

Often ADs are trying to save themselves through this work. This calling is their identity, and they cannot betray their identity. They ache to succeed.

We in the community are often happy to turn the responsibility for our kids' salvation over to them. In fact, as we outsource our kids' salvation, you can almost hear the sigh of relief among adults in our town.

Of course, it's not like we're doing nothing in return— Young Life asks us to help them, and we're happy to help. We pray and prepare dinners. We give money.

Results? That's not on our shoulders. We leave it to the experts.

 How do you view your personal responsibility for your town and your kids and their salvation?

WHO OWNS YOUR AREA?

While we often talk about Area authority, Area *ownership* isn't given much attention. At first glance they may seem the same, but the distinction has significant impact on the Area.

The Young Life Office of Global Innovation surveyed

nearly 1,200 YL Areas, asking, "Who owns your Area?" They asked respondents to select from three options:

1. the community
2. the Area Director
3. the Committee

Seventy-eight percent of respondents answered B, the Area Director.

Why is this important? Ownership is central to success. It determines where Volunteers decide their responsibilities begin and end. Committees are not generally aware of the "have no formal authority" restriction. At least in practice they do not operate in such a limited capacity. The practical operating limits come from this ownership question.

Ownership informs stopping points. Nonowners pick stopping points short of what owners pick. They don't study what owners study. They don't check what owners double- and triple-check.

If the AD owns the Area, he or she has "got this," right?

If the AD owns the Area, the community stands down.

Young Life isn't wrong. Our town is.

Look, there would be nothing wrong with outsourcing our kids' salvation if God wanted us to or would let us. Or maybe if *it worked*. But our kids are the responsibility of the adults in our town. Outsourcing doesn't work and he won't let us do it.

WHY CAN'T THE COMMUNITY'S GOD-GIVEN RESPONSIBILITY BE OUTSOURCED?

When I realized our town had outsourced our kids' salvation, God gave me these words: Our Town, Our Kids.

Our goal has been to be caring and responsible for the kids in our town.

Professionally, we accept the idea that if we are given an

important responsibility, we may be able to delegate some of the tasks but we can't delegate the ultimate responsibility. Why do we think we can do this spiritually?

The Bible tells parents their offspring are a reward from him (Psalms 127:3–5) and instructs parents further in the following verses:

> Start children off on the way they should go (Proverbs 22:6)

> Teach them to your children, talking about them when you sit at home and when you walk along the road, when you lie down and when you get up. (Deuteronomy 11:19)

No one can own this for us.

Look, I'm sure I'd love the kids of Toledo, Tel Aviv, or Toronto. But I do not ache for them equal to the way I ache for kids in IMYL. This must be part of God's plan. He put some of his people here for these kids. He put others there for those kids.

As a community we must come to terms with the truth that we have primary responsibility for creating the environment for the salvation of the kids in our town. We are grateful for Young Life, which serves as an experienced guide, but our town and our kids are our responsibility.

WHY DOES OUTSOURCING NOT WORK?

When we outsource our kids' salvation and delegate owner-ship to the AD, we limit ministry potential. Why? Because we have just benched the wisest souls in our town.

- The community has long-term relationships with churches, coaches, administrators, and youth pastors. An AD doesn't have the collective breadth of these relationships.

- The community has access to financial and business experience the ministry-focused AD may or may not possess.
- The community has lived and absorbed the history of the Area in ways the AD couldn't accomplish in decades.

It's impossible for an AD to have comparable knowledge to what the collective community already possesses. This isn't a slam on ADs; it's simply about numbers. We have ten thousand people living in our Area. We have one YL Area Director. You might have three or even more Staff members.

But there are *thousands* of trustworthy YL Volunteers in our mission who have never drawn a YL paycheck. Getting a YL paycheck is an incomplete way to evaluate skill or authority. Often the most trustworthy IMYL Volunteers have made enough mistakes along the way to gain wisdom. We need them applying their experience in our town for our kids. It is counterproductive to diminish their role simply because they are not YL Staff.

Areas owned by Area Directors often remain small. Too few people are engaged and responsible for Area health and growth. It's not the fault of the AD, but AD-owned Areas suffer limitations on ministry impact and outreach.

IS IT APPROPRIATE TO EXPLORE A NEW SCRIPT?

Past YL president Bob Mitchell told me YL Committees originated for financial support. They were for fund-raising, not soul raising—and there's a compelling explanation for this.

The script is from the 1940s and '50s. Companies and organizations adhered to a hierarchical structure. This was the approach taken by a tiny, unknown ministry called Young Life.

Leadership kept a tight grip lest the mission veer from the intended trajectory. They trusted themselves the most, and it's a good thing they did. The result was Young Life grew beyond everyone's dreams but God's.

The legacy model put the big work and big decisions in the hands of those who drew a YL paycheck and fund-raising in the hands of the Committee. It is now eighty years later. Today there is much more potential in Committees. The historical script built Young Life into a worldwide miracle. Our reimagined script reimagines Committees' potential in this global miracle today. Ideas developed in this book address Staff lonesomeness and reevaluating Committee potential. They have been successful for our Area. Implementing them on a broader scale is worthy of consideration.

In this chapter, we've talked about where God places responsibility for the salvation of our kids. We've talked about the resources and wisdom that often get missed in AD-owned Areas.

And there's something else that can go wrong when we outsource our kids' salvation. We're tempted to see YL as a provider. You know, like a supplier to a business. But this is not right either. Three painful outcomes occur when we treat YL like a business. We'll discuss these in the next chapter.

3

ARE YOU APPROACHING YOUR YL AREA LIKE A BUSINESS?

For all those who exalt themselves will be humbled, and those who humble themselves will be exalted.

— *Luke 18:14*

The Downing House, built in 1890, is a historical Denver and Young Life icon. Our Front Range regional Staff gather there monthly for a day consecrated for fellowship, the Word, and encouragement.

I often attended to learn and support Andy and the regional Staff.

One day I overheard an AD make an interesting comment about Committees and Committee Chairs. She warned, "When you're working with a Committee, watch out for the businessperson!"

She had a point. Many of us who are Committee Chairs and Committee members are also business experts. As businesspeople, we typically have experience managing people and improving operations. And because we're often working with Staff who don't have our experience, what we know really does help.

But her hesitancy starts to gain traction when we consider how, as businesspeople, we can approach YL like other businesses we have run. It's compulsive.

Our attention gravitates to efficiency, organization, and value. We want results, as does YL. And if results aren't clear, we try to figure out why.

> *She warned, "When you're working with a Committee, watch out for the businessperson!"*

In other words, we begin to think of YL as a vendor, as if we've purchased YL services and know-how to be used for our town. And no savvy businessperson is willing to pay for something and not get what they purchased, right?

I know I fell into the category. Out of habit, I applied what I knew from business to IMYL.

Unfortunately, it became a log in my eye.

A Young Life Area may look like a business, but it is not a business; it's a community. It's not even an organization—it's an organism, part of the body of Christ. It is the church ordained by God. It is "a community created by God in which we can participate."[1]

When we start thinking of YL as a business, we create problems. Let's look at four ministry-damaging dynamics that can occur.

1. AREA DIRECTORS ARE EXPECTED TO OPERATE LIKE BUSINESSPEOPLE.

Let me explain why applying business-world expectations to ADs doesn't work.

There's a reason ADs don't offer their skills to the performance-driven world of business. They go into YL because they are ministers of the gospel. Their choice to bring their gifts into the relationship-driven world of ministry is less a career move than a calling.

As a result, ADs may struggle in a hyperefficient business environment. More important, they may not feel comfortable revealing they're struggling. They push on alone, continuing to struggle in a transactional structure.

This doesn't happen because of lack of effort on the part of the AD. Area Directors are passionate about this work, and they work hard. This calling is their identity, and they cannot betray their identity. They ache to succeed.

And while businesspeople want to help Staff succeed, as Committee Chairs we tend to *manage* Staff more than *walk with them.*

2. AREA DIRECTORS END UP OVERWORKED AND LONESOME.

In a business model, we are paying the AD to do the job. Businesses pay people to do things, and ADs are paid professionals after all. This creates expectations.

The AD is the first one we seek when work beckons. We are helpers at best. This means we offer our help if we have the time, if we have the skills, and if we have the want-to.

As a result, ADs often end up responsible for events. Too often, ADs directly raise much of the money.

I've heard ADs say, "It's easier this way," but it's only because they, too, have bought into the leader-helper model. But the leader-helper model isolates ADs.

Andy tried so many times and in so many ways to tell me he was not doing okay.

He was becoming overwhelmed with fear and lonesomeness. The weight and pressures of what he had taken on began to keep him awake at night.

The organization continued to celebrate him and cheer him

on. But he didn't need employee-of-the-month accolades—he needed true partners in ministry.

Staff lonesomeness rooted in the leader-helper model is epidemic. The joy of the job often yields to despair.

This is a sin our town needed to recognize and own.

By seeing YL as a business, we flubbed a ministry.

3. RELATIONSHIPS AND CONNECTION ARE REPLACED BY EFFICIENCY AND PROCESS.

Businesses and organizations rely on visions, operations and processes to get stuff done.

Communities and organisms grow and connect.

Though not mutually exclusive, these are vastly different ways of operating.

After three years, our Area began to stumble. Staff members were not feeling healthy or successful. Our first instincts were not Christlike. Because we were treating YL like an organization, we addressed these problems by trying to improve our operations.

I'd ask Andy to do in a week more than he (or I) could have gotten done in six months.

We were as inept in assuming we'd get more out of our Volunteers.

How hard could it be? We simply needed to round up more people to do the work, right?

We overtapped seasoned Volunteers. We cajoled. We made phone calls that began with the words, "We need a meal for twelve Leaders and Staff. Would you organize this?" without enough consideration for the gifts, needs, or gratification of the individuals we were asking.

After all, if our goal was to get more done, we needed to focus on results. Our outsourcing mind-set led us down the road of treating ministry like a business run by paid Staff.

You can see why this can't work, but we didn't. Not at first.

We learned the hard way. After three years we began to see the limiting contours of our organizational focus. Intermountain Young Life was as dry as a January Christmas tree.

4. YOUNG LIFE IS TREATED AS AN ORGANIZATION, NOT AN ORGANISM.

Jesus treated the early church as the organism it is. He led His people with love and vision. He knew an organism moves like a school of fish: a push here, a nudge there. In contrast, I was narrowly focused and clumsy. Yes, I understand the ADs' lament, "Watch out for the businessperson." Regarding this, I'd now pray, "If you are a businessperson, be wise. Pull back the lens and make certain you aren't impeding even with your expertise and best of intentions."

Today the people in our town want to be part of something bigger than an organization could ever produce. We want order, of course, but not an organization. Today we strive to communicate needs, create opportunities, and trust the organism.

We do this by creating relationships. Volunteers get loved, not leveraged. We're dedicated to seeing Volunteers through the heart of Christ. Instead of *using* people, we strive to *honor* the gifts God has distributed to His people.

We approach Volunteers knowing they are seeking opportunities to grow in their faith. We seek these opportunities for them as well. The Volunteers, not the work, are our priority. If we are in it together, serving our town and our kids, we can complete any goal and do any project.

The same goes for our AD.

Loved, not leveraged.

We are not anchored in business ventures. We're liberated in ministry.

THREE SIGNS YOU THINK OF YOUNG LIFE AS A BUSINESS:

1. You try to make your ADs and Volunteers into your business image instead of recognizing them as bearers of the gospel answering a call from God.
2. You allow the impostor of performance to replace your community's love of Christ and kids.
3. You value your YL Area's efficiency over its relationships.

I was convinced my business skills were a contribution to our Area. I now view the greater context with gratitude. I was thirty degrees off course. There is room and glory for all our gifts if we get the posture and purpose right.

I had an incomplete sense of purpose. I fell into yet another ministry-damaging dynamic, which I'll share about in the next chapter.

4

ARE YOU FALLING INTO THE TRAP OF HIRING THEN BLAMING THE AD?

Therefore, as God's chosen people, holy and dearly loved, clothe yourselves with compassion, kindness, humility, gentleness and patience. Bear with each other and forgive one another if any of you has a grievance against someone. Forgive as the Lord forgave you.

— *Colossians 3:12–13*

My ham-fisted business advice didn't cure our decline after the years of early success. Tougher times were ahead, and I blamed Andy. How in the world did I justify blaming Andy?

Here's roughly how I formed my thoughts.

First, I saw our Area problems as local. (I now know all too well they're widespread.)

Some context may be useful. In our first years, our YL ministry proved shiny and attractive. New sells. Our town loved YL. Our kids loved YL. Camp sign-ups jumped. Club—perceived as new, creative, and fun—multiplied.

After a few years IMYL's local status shifted from new to respected. Respected in the community like the library, a burger shop, or the Chamber of Commerce. This is normal. It's a predictable shift from new to not new. I was aware of this well-known cycle but still succumbed to disappointment.

We congratulated ourselves too much for early success. Then we criticized ourselves too much for decline after three years. I was really frustrated. Ugh. We were not getting what we paid for.

One bad sunny, day I was driving back into the mountains after a difficult meeting where I was advised I was not being helpful to our YL Area. Of course, I rejected this accurate advice and returned to sorting out our local ministry. It felt small, dry. I felt beat-up and discouraged. The solution, the genuine partnership Andy and I needed, remained unrevealed.

I sat on a kitchen stool next to Jim and Ann Petzel, stalwarts of IMYL. They have profoundly shaped the ministry. Ann gave her all as a life-changing Leader for countless kids. Jim was our impassioned third Committee Chair. Jim recently read the Committee Handbook. He said, "We are just helpers here." I missed the chance to reimagine ourselves as more than helpers. I misused Jim's insight, and my misapplication was to blame Andy. This led to three serious negative outcomes. If you want to make sure your Area Director is lonesome, here are some field notes.

1. WE TRIED TO MANAGE AN "UNDERPERFORMING EMPLOYEE."

"We're producing a stagnant ministry," I told Andy. "I'm not seeing the effort needed."

We were sitting in his office. The tension was palpable.

"It's like this," I continued. "I've got my day job, and you have yours. I'll do mine; you do yours."

Andy and I were discussing the incomplete tasks that needed doing that week. Andy stared at me. He told me, "You and I want the same things for YL and for the community, but I'm not feeling loved."

It wasn't that I didn't love or want to love Andy. I did. But my focus was on IMYL's aging freshness. Decline was on us, and I thought better efforts were needed. By this I meant Andy's better efforts.

> *Young Life had six decades of experience. I expected Andy to draw on YL resources, fix the ministry, and keep it fixed.*

I was talking about fixing IMYL, and Andy was talking about love.

I had experienced this before. I broadly concluded Andy was an underperforming employee.

I unpacked my business tools. Concise words with crisp assignments. There we were, confronting the first friction in our relationship.

Andy was alone and sinking. Lucky for him, I chose to dole out plenty of business advice and direction.

I behaved as if loving Andy depended on his job performance. I came to see Andy was deeply influenced by his job performance as well. Performance anxiety is common for many of us. Young Life ADs are no exception.

Area Directors are often encouraged to separate their worth from their professional achievement (aren't we all?). Of course, it's easier said than done, and I sure wasn't helping with my transactional mind-set.

The psalmist writes, "Turn to me and be gracious to me, for I am lonely and afflicted" (Psalm 25:16).

Andy was asking for no more than this.

But I had other plans. I assumed Young Life would take responsibility for the Area Director's performance, that they would give him the training and guidance to produce greater results. After all, YL had six decades of experience. I expected

Andy to draw on YL resources, fix the ministry, and keep it fixed.

There is always a problem behind the problem. It now came into focus. Our Regional Director had over thirty direct reports. In my corporate life I was responsible for lots of people but rarely had more than six direct reports.

With six, you have the capacity to develop those six people. With a thirty-to-one ratio, professional development—not to mention soul care—becomes impractical.

The ratio alone showed our role had to include managing, guiding, and developing Andy. If we didn't step in, it wouldn't happen.

It's the ratio. It's the distance. It's the frequency. The ministry was not at the regional office. It was right here in our town.

We started to wake from our slumber.

2. WE NEGLECTED TO CONSIDER THE HOLY POSITION OF THE AD.

Area Directors are not looking for a job. They get called by God to ministry.

And while we as parents and community members often see the position of Area Director as holy in theory, we tend to miss it in practice. Andy saw himself as a called, obedient minister of the gospel. I would have said I did, too, but my actions told another story.

I had begun to *manage* a minister of the gospel. Jesus had a far better approach. He prayed for His disciples, led, and loved them. He lovingly and generously forgave them way past 490.

Furthermore, he made sure they weren't alone.

Jesus didn't send people out alone or to be alone. He sent them in pairs (Mark 6:7; Luke 10:1).

Andy needed me. I was uniquely positioned to be an equal

partner. I wouldn't learn how to be such a partner until three more years.

Eventually God would speak to me. Eventually He would clear up my perspective. The truth is, my business expectations were counterproductive. My transactional posture placed Andy in an employee status. This was my basis for operating. I stumbled because I replaced God's spiritual wishes with my professional experience.

3. WE LOOKED FOR VILLAINS—UNTIL WE REALIZED THERE WEREN'T ANY.

When we finally woke up, it was shattering.

Individual frictions are often symptomatic of larger organizational design issues. A *hire the Area Director and blame them* attitude causes plenty of friction.

Our fresh eyes arrived.

Turns out, there are no villains. Just actors in a play. The AD fails to follow the script the community imagines. The community fails to follow the script the AD has in their head. We blame each other, but as actors with different scripts, we keep friction on a low boil.

And Jesus weeps.

When the Spirit of truth comes, he will guide you into all truth. (John 16:13 NLT)

It would take tremendous pain and hardship before I submitted and humbled myself to my Lord. Andy did the same. God spoke to both of us the same day.

This wasn't solved through tasks, assignments, professional development, or pep talks. It was solved by and through Jesus Christ with mutual trust between Andy and me.

God was crystal clear to both of us: we needed a different relationship. An important relationship.

5

ARE YOU RECOGNIZING THE MOST IMPORTANT RELATIONSHIP IN THE AREA?

"Mitch, get out to California and get something going!"

—YL founder Jim Rayburn, 1956

Bob "Mitch" Mitchell and Claudia Mitchell have been friends to thousands in YL. They have inspired millions. Mitch was

Young Life's third president. But his introduction to Young Life began much sooner.

At thirteen Mitch was one of the first kids under Jim Rayburn's visionary leadership in the Dallas tent meetings.

> **God's answer, His gift, came wrapped in skin. He sent Mitch a friend.**

Mitch joined the YL Staff and took on every assignment available. He was YL's first wrangler, saddling horses and telling the kids to bring them back before supper.

Mitch could do anything.

Then one day he was issued a humbling challenge.

YL founder Jim Rayburn told him, "Go out to California and get something going!"

Mitch accepted an AD position in California, and he and his wife, Claudia, made the move. Upon their arrival, though, Mitch felt overwhelmed by the San Francisco Bay area. Overwhelmed by the task ahead.

One night he stood, cold and lonesome, on a windy San Francisco hillside. Looking at the city lights below, he began to cry. He didn't have a clue where or how he could begin to fulfill Rayburn's charge.

Rayburn had modeled the absolute necessity for prayer. Mitch and Rayburn had spent many nights in prayer meetings interceding for kids, camps, funds, and new Leaders.

Now, Mitch knew, if the mission were to grow, it had to depend on prayer. On that hillside, Mitch once again turned to God and asked for help.

In the coming days and weeks, Mitch wondered how God would answer his prayer. Would He inspire Mitch with newfound fortitude and perseverance? Would He empower Mitch to carry the load? After all, this is what many Young Life Staff people did then and still do today. They simply shoulder the burden and keep going.

But this wasn't God's answer at all. God's answer, His gift, came wrapped in skin. He sent Mitch a friend.

Meet Ted Johnson.

Ted says, "The first time I heard about Young Life was back in 1953 in the San Francisco Bay area. I was a rookie IBM salesman, and the salesman sitting next to me said, 'You ought to get involved with this Young Life thing.' I said, 'I just bought ten thousand dollars' worth of Penn Mutual. I don't need any more life insurance.' Then he tried to explain it to me, and I knew I wasn't interested, because I guess I was what you'd call one of those 'church disinterested' adults."

Ted adds, "Later my wife and I were snookered into chaperoning a busload of kids from Berkeley High School to Malibu in Canada, where we were Young Life's guests for a week. Bob Mitchell said he'd put me on the best salmon water in North America, and I didn't have to go to any meetings, attend any meals, just show up on the bus when it left Berkeley. Well, that week at Malibu cost me everything I have, including my day job!"

Ted explains that what he discovered in Malibu was "absolutely the best mission to which I could commit my life, my money, and everything we have."

Back home he asked Mitch what he could do to help.

"Join the Young Life Committee," Mitch answered.

"What's that?'

"Well, come to Wilkinson's Restaurant next Tuesday morning at seven o'clock for breakfast and you can find out. The Committee will be there. I'll introduce you, and by the way, would you be chairman?

Ted eventually became the Berkeley, California, Committee Chair. Later he chaired four other Committees. Ted's gifts included those of an organizer and raconteur.

While Mitch was maxed out using his gifts of speaking and teaching, Ted stayed busy coming up with new ways of telling the story of Young Life.

Take the pig-kissing contest, for instance. The idea was to see which Leaders—the girls' Leaders or the boys' Leaders—could bring the most kids to Club. Whoever lost would have to kiss a little piglet. The event was in Orinda, California, and the girls' Leaders lost. Mitch purchased a piglet in the spring. By fall it was a huge hog, and the kiss turned into a bite requiring stitches and a medical report. The puzzled insurance company questioned the claim but paid it anyway.

This was all Mitch was willing to reveal about the incident except to say, "We learned some lessons." Ted, on the other hand, held nothing back. Their stories of adventures and misadventures had you belly laughing in a heartbeat.

Ted also had a gift for ideas and an incredible knack for selling those ideas to the Area.

"Let's sell a week of Young Life!" he said during one brainstorming meeting. Then he divided the Area budget and sold it to donors in seven-day increments.

"Monday is Club, Tuesday is Campaigners, Friday is taking kids to football games," Ted explained to anyone willing to listen. "Sunday is the cherry on top when YL kids get to join the community in experiencing Mitch's teaching at Berkeley Presbyterian Church."

Donors didn't just write a check for the budget; they bought something they loved: a day or week (or more) of ministry.

Ted knew how to get people excited about Young Life and the Area.

Ted's arrival made all the difference. Ted and Mitch became inseparable through a friendship of mutual trust. The integration of their gifts ignited opportunities and enthusiastic community involvement.

Young Life experienced what the Area Director and Committee Chair relationship could be.

Ted speculated on his legacy: "As Committee Chairman, I want to give everything I can give. Not just my money, but I want to give myself. I want to encourage Mitch any way I can. I want to invest in this baby. I want to spend myself down to my last whatever-I-can-give. I want to write big checks, and I want the last check to bounce!"

Mitch was grateful to have a friend. He had Ted alongside to process successes, disappointments, problems, and solutions. They dealt with emotions and situations. They carried it all as one with Young Life's stylish sense of humor.

Mitch encouraged Ted to lead a Club, which he did.

Ted was all in.

As Ken "Tank" Tankersley once said, "If you have had your own encounter with Ted, then you completely understand why he was fondly described as YL's CEO—chief encouragement officer. You left every interaction feeling smarter, taller, funnier, wiser, and a better golfer then you were just moments earlier. He just had that gift."[1]

Ted left for his heavenly home in December of 2020. Mitch joined him in May of 2021. These two old friends were bound in trust and faith to serve Christ and kids—and now they are either on the second hole of a heavenly golf course or laughing as they reel in a big sockeye.

Some people are bigger than life.

Mitch and Ted. A real pair.

Their relationship was the most important relationship for each other and for the Area.

Andy and I were not a real pair. Not like Mitch and Ted.

Mitch and Ted had the priceless value of the unbreakable relationship figured out decades ago, and it lasted a lifetime.

Andy and I were only paired.

Is an unbreakable AD-CC relationship common? No, not common.

But there was a time two-by-two relationships were common.

God had seen and solved the weakness of one and the

strength of two before. In Mark 6:7 we read that "he began to send them out two by two."

> 66   *As Committee Chairman, I want to give everything I can give. Not just my money, but I want to give myself. I want to encourage Mitch any way I can.* — Ted Johnson

Andy arrived professionally alone, and it stayed that way for years. At first it didn't hurt him. He was surrounded and loved by our town. Eventually, however, anyone can become lonesome even in a crowd.

> Two are better than one, because they have a good
> return for their labor: If either of them falls down, one
> can help the other up. But pity anyone who falls and
> has no one to help them up. (Ecclesiastes 4:8)

In the foreword to this book, Andy shared that as he was mopping the floor, he was arguing with me in his mind. The Holy Spirit prompted him to pick up the phone, call me, and apologize. At this moment, God had been speaking to my heart too.

He called us to be the people He made us to be. He asked us to be patient and kind with each other.

He shouldn't have had to ask.

"Andy," I told him when he phoned, "I've created so much damage. I have reasons which seemed right to me, but they weren't. I am so sorry. If you'll let me, I want to reestablish trust with you. I know it will take a long time, but I think we can get there."

I could only hope, because expecting him to trust me at this point would have been audacious.

But this is where God was leading us.

God didn't want our efforts at compromise. He didn't want

my best or Andy's best apart from each other. He wanted our combined best as two strands to weave with his own for a lifetime bond.

For years, it never crossed my mind to question the YL policy of AD authority. I committed to the leader-helper model. But as Andy's and my relationship buckled, we strayed, thankfully, into evaluating the practice of AD authority. This peek at the relational problem behind the problem wasn't to be novel, iconoclastic, or revolutionary. Even to this day, our goal has never been to challenge or change Young Life.

All we knew is what we were doing in IMYL was not working. Lonesomeness shackled Andy. I was adding to the burden. We needed help.

We listened. We never could have done it on our own. The choice God gave us was simple: continue in disobedience, or trust and obey Him. These were our only options. We either were going to go our separate ways, or we were going to find a way—with and through Christ—to work together.

We've shed tears. We've reconciled. Our relationship was transfigured.

After seven years God made our bond into what should have been set in motion in the first ten minutes.

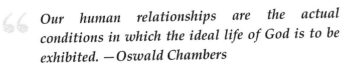

Our human relationships are the actual conditions in which the ideal life of God is to be exhibited. —Oswald Chambers

I wish we hadn't been clueless in those first ten minutes about outsourcing our kids' salvation. I wish we had known going in pairs was so necessary. So fruitful. In our adult wisdom we never should have let the first ten minutes usher our town and Young Life into parallel tracks. We never should have let our excited Andy take on so much and our enthusiastic town take on so little.

Transformation took years. We shaped our future with the expertise, traditions, and know-how of Young Life. We experienced the joy of relationship and actual partnership. Today Andy Morman is one of my favorite people on the planet. I am one of his. And Genna even likes me now. Bless you, Genna Morman.

> " *We designed our future: 100 percent indivisible joint responsibility for everything that happens in our Area.*

Oswald Chambers said, "Our human relationships are the actual conditions in which the ideal life of God is to be exhibited." Well, ours was not the ideal life, and maybe we had to go this way. But I don't think so. We can establish Areas better up front.

To be sure, good ministry happens in the YL leader-helper model. Kids do meet Jesus, as attested to by millions of changed lives, including mine. But a caution here. Assigning formal authority to the AD for consistency and order has unintended consequences. Disproportionate responsibility falls on the shoulders of the Area Director. Too many ADs feel isolated and lonesome. The leader-helper model tends to create lonesomeness. As Andy and I reevaluated the AD-CC relationship, we submitted to Christ in our desire to be better leaders.

In other words, we embraced a modernized version of the model lived out by Bob Mitchell and Ted Johnson.

As a result, we began to experience better coordination, better decision making, better leadership.

Over a couple of years, trust returned. Companionship replaced lonesomeness.

We designed our future: 100 percent indivisible joint responsibility for everything that happens in our Area.

In my AD-CC relationship with Andy there is no division of responsibilities. Together we work out with the community what the priorities are. We collaborate to address those priorities.

Now, don't miss this: indivisible responsibility does not mean fifty-fifty labor. After all, Andy had a full-time paid position in IMYL and I did not. We divided our efforts with this in mind. Labor and hard work had never been our central problems.

The point is our reimagined relationship solved the problem of AD lonesomeness. It removed the burden of Andy feeling overwhelmed. Our restructured relationship yielded freedom and life.

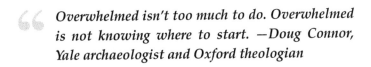

> *Overwhelmed isn't too much to do. Overwhelmed is not knowing where to start.* —*Doug Connor, Yale archaeologist and Oxford theologian*

Many YL Area Directors and Committee Chairs have had similarly contentious experiences. This is why Andy and I have traveled the country telling our story.

Our story concludes with many years of health. Andy is not lonesome. I am not lonesome. A partnership devoid of fear and lonesomeness unlocked freedom and health for us.

Cindy Yohann heard us tell our story in Spokane. Her reaction was to capture Andy's and my future as "a relationship strong enough to bear the weight of the opportunity."

6

ARE YOU INVITING VOLUNTEERS
TO JOIN A STORY?

*Do nothing out of selfish ambition or vain conceit. Rather, in
humility value others above yourselves, not looking to your own
interests but each of you to the interests of the others.*

—*Philippians 2:3–4*

It's possible good organizations send you emails with subject
lines like these:

"We need help with . . ."

"Donate Now!"

"Can you help us?"

These organizations and ministries tell me what I can do
for them. Often, I'm asked for money as they invite me to help
fund their story.

Many of these groups are doing important things. Still, I
rarely act on this organizationally self-centered approach.

Just because a ministry is doing good work doesn't mean
people will automatically feel moved to contribute to their
story.

The same goes for YL.

In the worldwide YL mission of over a hundred countries, there are five thousand paid Staff and eighty-six thousand Volunteers.

Five thousand Staff. A lot of people.

Eighty-six thousand Volunteers. A lot more people.

Keep those numbers in mind.

So why is good help so hard to find?

To be clear, I am not talking about Leaders in direct ministry working with kids. That's another book, and they are hard to find.

I'm talking about the community group of Volunteers. These are the people who pray, serve on Committee, make meals, and fill tables for the banquet.

I've heard a lot of glib explanations about people being overcommitted, too busy, or uncaring. If help seems hard to find, in our experience it isn't for lack of willing and capable people looking for meaning and purpose.

What are the root causes of Volunteer shortages? What changes can we make to help us find the Volunteers needed for the next twenty years?

THE ASYMMETRY OF STAFF AND VOLUNTEERS

Area Directors across the country have told us, "I'm afraid to ask too much of our Volunteers because I'm afraid they will leave."

In the leader-helper model, ADs adopt a Volunteer scarcity mind-set and pull their punches. They don't want to scare off Volunteers.

When an AD is overworked and feels like quitting, there are barriers. It takes time to secure the next position. Becoming frustrated or bored and moving on isn't easily done.

Boom. Stuck.

But when a YL Volunteer feels like quitting, it's another

story. Some Volunteers join and stay like glue. Most Volunteers shift interest and move on. They reason to themselves, *I've done my bit for Young Life. It's somebody else's turn.*

> *Five thousand Staff. A lot of people.*
> *Eighty-six thousand Volunteers. A lot more people.*
> *Keep those numbers in mind.*

Unlike the AD, Volunteers are not fastened to YL. Leaving does not plunge them into financial hardship or career crisis. They must merely summon an explanation to placate the Area Director. "I've taken on more responsibility at the office" usually does it. Their obligations to YL are informal at best. They can leave anytime. Like right now.

Boom. Free.

This reveals the asymmetry of Staff and Volunteers. Staff can feel too trapped as they watch Volunteers feel too free.

This perpetuates the idea that Volunteers are helpers for Young Life, not warriors for our town and our kids. Once again, the leader-helper model is creating problems.

This asymmetry seems intractable, but it isn't. Healthy and productive AD-Volunteer symmetry *is* obtainable.

ROMANCING OUR COMMUNITY INTO THE "OUR TOWN, OUR KIDS" STORY

How do you get Volunteers to grasp the bigger picture? Change their posture? Make a lasting commitment to our town and our kids instead of a short-lived commitment to Young Life?

You don't. Christ does. After all, it's His story, His kids.

But this doesn't mean there aren't practical things you can do that will help people catch the vision. Here are five road-tested actions you can take:

. . .

1. Model AD-CC leadership that is strong and united.

Volunteers want to follow good leadership. Seeing united, loving leadership in the Area is attractive and inspiring.

This, as you can imagine, adds another dimension to the value of the most important relationship in the Area, the AD-CC relationship.

The relationship of the AD and CC demonstrates the story you're inviting Volunteers to join.

Support each other enthusiastically when you are together and when you are apart. Always reinforce your mutual commitment to our town and our kids. Don't criticize your partner to others but raise any concerns privately with your partner and work things out confidentially. Make this your motto: "Less of me, Lord. More of you." As Jesus Himself said, "Come, follow me, . . . and I will send you out to fish for people" (Matthew 4:19).

Every time the AD and CC speak, they should take the opportunity to reinforce the power of the "Our Town, Our Kids" message.

The CC can always shower Young Life and the AD with community gratitude for teaching us to fish.

This isn't about leaders and helpers, tasks, or to-dos. This is about coming together in commitment and relationship for a greater good. It's our town taking personal responsibility for our kids.

With this kind of unified commitment, people in your community will notice. They'll want to be a part of what they're seeing.

2. Give Volunteers what they want—and it's not "less work."

It's no secret each of us longs to be known and longs for lives filled with purpose.

Volunteers are no different.

Young Life doesn't need Volunteers as much as Volunteers need opportunities. They'll make a meaningful difference in our towns by using their gifts and skills. We don't "use" Volunteers—or anyone else. Using people violates our core values—and it is counterproductive. Volunteers are not the *labor* that makes it possible for Area leadership to do glorious YL work. Better, their efforts are a direct line into our kids' lives and need to be recognized as such. We challenge ourselves in each instance, *Are we using this person or providing a blessing?*

If Volunteers are not stepping up with what you need, you may be tempted to ask yourself, *Who are these lazy people?*

These "lazy" people started the soccer league. They led the effort for the high school physics lab. They built the new baseball diamond. They founded the bank—or started the GoFundMe campaign—that paid for these projects.

They are leaders in their churches. They are movers and shakers with the chamber of commerce. They speak at Rotary, donate to the Salvation Army, the Children's Hospital, and other nonprofits. They *do* have lives of meaning, and they Volunteer where they can make a difference. They are looking to do more, not less.

They may be a subset of the town, but there are plenty of them.

Our opportunity is to match them with opportunities to change the world for our kids, one kid at a time. This might mean providing a meal, being a Leader, or writing a check so the next kid can hear the gospel straight.

They built and continue to build our towns. We can't be afraid to ask too much because they might leave.

3. Tap into the wisdom that Volunteers long to share.

Community wisdom has experiential and historical components. For example, our town was founded 170 years ago, in the mid-nineteenth century. We have people who have lived here for seventy years and many more who have lived here for twenty years or more.

Area Directors are rarely here more than five to ten years.

Locals know about unresolved church schisms, pastor experiences, and gifting opportunities.

They attended the high school when it was on the other side of town. They know the principal used to give only secular organizations permission to meet on campus because churches pushed too hard. They settled their hearts and refined their approach.

They know the most active bar in town is the relocated original Episcopal church. They have pictures of it rolling downtown on logs in the 1920s. They can connect people with a phone call. They know why the drug rehab facility had to leave town. They know why this next one will succeed.

They know *so* much.

4. Invest in relationships with kids, yes, but crucially with adults in your town.

At YL, we create relationships. This is our core competency. We are best in class.

How does a kid find Christ? In many cases, it's because of a relationship with a Leader. Befriending kids is hard work over a long time. Kids owe us nothing. We owe them everything. If they leave our town without hearing the gospel straight, we have let them down. The Barna organization tells us that kids thirteen to seventeen are unlikely to come to know Christ if our town squanders those ages, yet over half of teens want to learn more about Jesus. [1] These years are when they are learning and gathering their essentials for life. We must use these precious years and build relationships with kids.

Befriending adults is hard work over a long time. Adults care about our town, but they don't know us.

And how does an adult find meaning as a Volunteer in our Area? In many cases, they are introduced to the idea because they have a relationship with a YL community member, Volunteer, or YL Staff member.

If we want to attract engaged and committed Volunteers, we must apply what we know about kids to adults.

A Young Life kid and now local pastor Jason Freeman created the large photo featured below. Adults in his Bergen Park Church congregation find familiar faces in the photo. The picture is a great conversation starter.

Befriending adults is hard work over a long time. Adults care about our town, but they don't know us. They owe our ministry nothing. We must make the same effort with adults that we make with kids. Probably more. We must earn the right to be heard and scrub our minds mind from thinking anybody owes us anything. They owe us nothing. Nothing. We are in ministry. We owe others everything.

Relationships are our superpower. Get to know people in your town. Meet with them and ask them to tell their stories. Rip up your agenda, your needs, your offer for them to help us or donate. Build relationships and spread joy for its own sake. Pursue the hearts of adults just like you pursue the hearts of kids; then let God take the wheel. Don't choose between our town and our kids.

We have so much to offer adults: life, meaning, satisfaction, contribution, legacy.

But we can't offer these things to people with whom we don't have relationships.

Adults are big kids. I, for instance, am still an eight-year-old kid. I want friendships, relationships. I'm not desperate. I'm not needy. I want to be known. I want to be a contributor to my community. I'll putter in my garage if you don't make the effort to know me and my story. But when you do, I light up like the kid I am. It might be you who helps me find or grow my faith.

5. Understand people in your town long to be invited to join the big story of Christ and kids.

Nix the requests that begin with the words *We need* or *Here's how you can help.*

When we talk to potential Volunteers, we focus on the longing within us all to be known. We know they want to play a part in something bigger than themselves. We figure out our needs later. Obligations, assigned duties, and seats on the bus are transactional buzzkills.

But when we invite someone to "be Christ to our town," this stirs the heart.

Change the invitation. How? Consider this example:

"Only if it would bless you, would you consider assisting Sharon with the banquet? We're inviting you because we think you'd be blessed by the opportunity."

This is an approach that takes people's eyes off their shoes. Encourage them to say no if the opportunity doesn't fit their desires, season, or schedule. Encourage them to decline if it doesn't seem like a blessing. Will doing so leave you in a lurch? Our experience says no. God has always provided for His people, and He always will. If it takes a little longer to find the person who would be blessed, we've done the right thing.

We long to be part of an important story. There is no doubt our towns and YL are part of an important story.

Our town is not building Young Life. Our town is gratefully walking with Young Life as we romance the love of Christ to our kids.

Earlier I talked about organizations inviting me to support their ministry story. I said they rarely move me to show up for a work day or reach for my Cash App.

Volunteers don't want to be a peripheral part of someone else's story. They want to play a meaningful role in a story they can make stronger and make their own. Our towns and YL Areas have a *great* story to invite Volunteers to join.

You might be thinking something along these lines: *This Volunteering approach sounds promising. Right now I'm interested in how do you do run day-to-day operations?*

To get you started, we have a serviceable model to share. We're confident you'll develop your own content and cadence —but this will get you going; then please share your improvements with us.

ARE YOU INTERESTED IN OUR
APPROACH TO A HEALTHY AREA?

Do your best to present yourself to God as one approved, a worker who does not need to be ashamed and who correctly handles the word of truth.

—*2 Timothy 2:15*

Andy and I were sitting at the Muddy Buck in downtown Evergreen. We came here every Tuesday at nine a.m. We were enjoying our usual—an Americano for Andy and a sturdy coffee, black, for me. We were smiling. It had been a good week.

We rarely had anything but good weeks. Our conversation over coffee reflected this.

If you happened to be sitting at the table next to us, here are a few snippets of conversation you might have overheard:

"How was Club last night?"

"We laughed hard with forty-six kids. And early camp sign-ups are ahead of schedule, with twenty down payments already in."

"Eric, will you pray for us this morning?"

"Lord, hear our prayer for kids so they may . . ."

"What are you afraid of today, Andy?"

"Nothing."

"Eric, what are you afraid of today?"

"We're a little behind on the banquet team. Sharon has most of her team assembled but lost one along the way. The Lake House is safely booked. But the bridge still isn't under reconstruction, so the event location is still at risk. With Sharon Regan Williams in charge, I'm never too afraid, but it's on my mind."

Our sacrosanct weekly meeting is a highlight of my week. I love being Committee Chair, and I love Andy.

Our town, our kids. Ours is ours. Young Life and the community are responsible for ministry together.

Sure, sometimes there are problems to solve, and when there are, we solve them together. If the CC breaks it, *we* fix it. If the AD breaks it, *we* fix it. If somebody from across the planet breaks it, *we* fix it. Together. No division of responsibility.

No blame. Lots of fix.

Did it happen overnight? No.

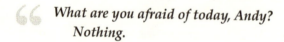

What are you afraid of today, Andy?
Nothing.

HOW ANDY AND I GOT BACK ON TRACK

I was driving in the car navigating one of a thousand mountain curves in Evergreen. The phone rang. I picked up. It was Andy.

We were still exploring each other in the new world into which God had invited us. The days of bad calls were done, but we weren't at the point of good calls yet.

Andy was checking in, but in a few minutes, he got to the real point.

"Eric, deep down I'm afraid to let go of the pain and make

a new future. I don't like admitting it, but this is real. We have a huge opportunity, and our coming together is going to happen. But trust comes one thin layer at a time."

"Andy, I have the same concern. The great thing is I completely believe we are going to get there. But like you said, it can't be granted; it must be built, which means we must be patient."

With the shared goal of reconciliation, we began to establish each vital layer of trust. First came personal trust followed by trust from Andy's family. Professional trust came next as we focused on our town and our kids.

Our mutually inflicted pain during our falling out needed time to heal. There were hard memories, but healing continued to bless us.

Reconstituted as a pair, we began to experience new power. In a triple strand with Christ, our strength became secure.

We still had fears. Hiding fears in an Area is common. Area Directors try to fix problems before they become known to the Committee Chair or the Committee. Without trust, we operate in fear while trying to stay ahead of the problem.

Yet the Lord continued to show Andy and me—indeed, He shows all of us — you can't do ministry very well in fear.

For God has not given us a spirit of fear, but of power
and of love and of a sound mind. (2 Timothy 1:7 NKJV)

We resolved to go straight through the front door. We would identify our fears and solve them together.

How?

We departed the leader-helper model. We acknowledged God had not given us a spirit of fear. Because it seemed so right, we became actual partners. Equal partners.

The Lone Ranger was a TV cowboy in the time of early Westerns. He had a silver bullet with marvelous qualities that helped him get out of trouble. What Andy and I didn't realize for a long time was we had a silver bullet too. This silver bullet was relationship.

In our Area, we protect and maximize two key relationships:

1. the relationship between the AD and the CC
2. our relationship with our community and Volunteers

What Is the "Our Town, Our Kids" Area Model?

- A complete marriage between the organization of Young Life and Our Town.
- The Area Director and Committee Chair indivisibly lead the area with 100 percent shared responsibility.
- Young Life deploys its toolkit through a minister of the gospel, the Area Director.
- Our town provides its wisdom, resources, and scalable labor.
- Our inseparable focal point is Christ and kids.

WE OPERATE AS AN AD-CC TEAM, AS EQUAL PARTNERS

Protecting and maximizing the relationship between the AD and the CC means intentional conversation. Equal partnership is less complicated. It is ours. Not Andy's, not mine. Ours. Complicated comes from assumptions like, "Hey, I thought *you* were going to take responsibility for that issue."

In most ways equal is easier. In every way equal is better.

We commit to meet face-to-face every week for an hour, same time, same place; we are perpetually building trust.

A common misunderstanding of becoming equal partners is that the time commitment is much larger on the Committee Chair's part. This has not been my experience. Because of our trust, common knowledge from our weekly meetings, coordination does not take lots of time. And our relationship is joyful, not fearful. The power of the 100 percent partnership model is not in the division of labor but in the indivisibility of responsibility.

Our weekly meeting has a structured format. Here's what we do:

1. We pray together.

We pray for our town, then our kids and for each other and our families.

2. We take turns asking each other, "What are you most afraid of?"

If we are fearful, ministry will suffer. We are people, and we have fears. We reveal our fears to each other. The question "What are you afraid of?" is the primary catalyst for agenda items. Communicating our fears is our most important work in the hour.

"I'm afraid if we lose another Leader, Campaigners will suffer."

"I'm afraid we'll be in deficit in February, and the banquet isn't until April."

"I'm afraid the new principal will restrict Leaders from campus."

We solve the fear or at least acknowledge and address it. We cannot do ministry if we are not honest about what is making our stomachs upset. You can't do ministry well if you don't believe your partner (AD or CC) honors your fears and will address them with you. Oh how I wish my corporate bosses had created an atmosphere where I could share my fears and they'd hear them and have my back.

Our discussion of fears is primarily Area-focused but not always. Some fears stem from world events or issues with our loved ones or health. We talk about these, too, and provide comfort even if a solution is not at hand.

Fear stops ministry, creates shame, and creates guilt. We

acknowledge and address fears and own them together 100 percent.

Most of the fear magically goes away because we know we are not alone. We aren't hiding the fears. We have a partner who owns our fears with us. Solving one or more fears creates success for every hour we spend together. Destroying fear together polishes the silver bullet.

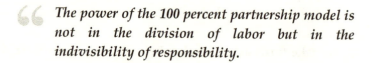

> *The power of the 100 percent partnership model is not in the division of labor but in the indivisibility of responsibility.*

3. We solve, we create, and we work.

There is still a ton of work to do. Whew. Area Directors and Committee Chairs are not afraid of work. Young Life Staff is not afraid of work. The burden comes from being alone and uncertain about what to do. The weight comes from being afraid somebody will find out the truth about our fears. We smoke out the fears and fix them together.

Or if we can't figure out together how to fix it, we find someone in the community who can.

Fear is the enemy, not work.

Each week we review progress on existing projects. We also confirm our priorities as we allocate limited resources to the most impactful projects.

4. We do not distinguish between the Committee handbooks' "day-to-day activities" and "long-range, major decision making."

Staff lonesomeness stems far more from day-to-day activities than long-range, major decision making.

5. Clarity on 100 percent joint responsibility between the AD and CC must be established ASAP (and extra points if it is in the first ten minutes).

Done collaboratively, 100 percent joint responsibility is not intrusive. It is healthy. It makes us more of a community.

6. We laugh and encourage.

Every time we meet, we share the fellowship of leading together and recognizing we are neither all-knowing nor alone. We pray and head out.

7. We find ways to professionally develop our Staff.

The Committee Chair keeps an eye on Staff careers, i.e., the talented ministers of the gospel who honor us with the next step in their life and career. They can expect to become more valuable professionals through their experience in IMYL. We don't use Area Directors and other Staff; we develop them.

Many Committee Chairs have led and developed talent in the business world. It is our responsibility to do the same for our Staff. We teach them the unglamorous aspects of being a leader.

Meetings run on schedule and according to preset agendas in order to show respect for all IMYL. Staff learn this helps to avoid drying out ministry. It organizes and focuses discussion and solutions.

> *Often there is a wide gap in expectations that identifies the problem behind the problem.*

We coach interactions with community, Volunteers, the Young Life organization, and policies. We coach interactions with Leaders, donors, churches, school Staff, and other IMYL Staff.

We discuss teamwork, emotional intelligence, and leadership. We practice accountability, prioritization, motivation, and creativity. We expect empathy. We teach effective communication. We use the extraordinary book *Crucial Conversations: Tools for Talking When Stakes Are High.*[1]

So often our fears, our insidious fears, are rooted in a lack of specific professional development.

8. Our annual performance is reviewed jointly as an AD-CC unit.

We want to be identified by our community and our region as being spiritually paired. As an extension, we ask our Regional Director to review our performance together. This reflects (and confirms) our 100 percent joint responsibility. Historically, the AD provides most of the input into their own review, and the CC can contribute as well. This is not the case in IMYL. We cherish our joint review. It strengthens and bonds us.

> **ESSENTIAL ACTIVITY:** Carve out two hours. As AD and CC, separate for thirty minutes and write down your expectations of your counterpart. For example, "I expect you to . . ." Complete the list, exchange, and discuss. This may save your friendship, and it may save your Area. It will save you years. Andy and I have never seen an AD and CC write down the same expectations.

Often there is a wide gap in expectations that identifies the problem behind the problem.

HOW WE LEAD AND ENGAGE OUR YL COMMUNITY

We put a lot of thought and intention into protecting and maximizing our AD-CC partner relationship. Our relationships with our community and with Volunteers require nothing less. Here's how we do it:

1. We pray.

> Your love has given me great joy and encouragement, because you, brother, have refreshed the hearts of the Lord's people. (Philemon 1:7)

We invite our town and our kids and our Leaders to pray every day. We invite people to set an alarm every day to pray in fellowship. One of our founding couples started the plan, and phones buzz in the pockets across our entire town every evening. We pray as a community for our town and our kids. If you're out and about, let your alarm trigger some great conversations. Skeptics are particularly intrigued.

Hundreds of alarms are set so we corporately pray for our town and our kids at 5:55 p.m. every day.

 Embracing sublime inefficiency could be our most effective innovation for building community.

2. We adhere to the following IMYL values:

- We build relationships with adults as we do with students—with no agenda.
- We don't *use* anybody for anything at any time. We invite. "Only if it would bless you, would you be interested in working on the Christmas party?" We trust God to send the people. We pray assured of abundance, not afraid of scarcity.
- We celebrate each Staff member and Volunteer when they arrive. We celebrate them while they are here. We celebrate them when they leave. We do not tug on Staff or Volunteers or hold on to them if it is time to leave. We trust their decision and trust God will send their replacement. He always does.
- We are very *efficient* with our administrative time. We get our administrative work done quickly so we can be in the community with kids and adults.
- We are very *inefficient* with relationships. We celebrate time well wasted. Relationships are inefficient by their nature.

Paul instructs us, "Do not conform to the pattern of this world" (Romans 12:2).

Embracing sublime inefficiency could be our most effective innovation for building community.

It certainly differentiates us and positions us in the world but not of the world.

3. We work through work crews.

We involve the community with purpose and intention.

We have dissolved traditional Committee. We don't meet once a month. I would be happy to show you all the letters complaining about not meeting once each month, but I never got any.

People in our town like projects with a duration and an outcome. They don't like standing committees. Our Area has less operational work than you'd think. Most traditional Committees are standing armies. They spend their time polishing their guns but don't often take up arms.

We experimented with more meetings. Then fewer meetings. Next, meetings with dinner and spouses. Meetings offsite, meetings with wine, meetings with dessert. We had movers, shakers, and builders sitting around in a circle staring at their shoes. The routine uninspiring meetings themselves were the problem. Neither wines nor desserts nor any other factor ever made the meetings much better. Why? Because there isn't that much to do.

Projects with a deliverable outcome solved most of what we had to do. These projects created the benefit of involving more people for less time.

Here are examples of our IMYL work crews:

- Leader Care
- Financial Durability
- Community
- Events
- Team YL (bicycle fellowship and fund-raiser)
- Digital Community and Branding
- Church Relationships

We address episodic and ongoing responsibilities through work crews. You know, like YL camp. Organizing a work crew happens through a work crew boss. We ask the work crew boss to accept or define a project with a deliverable outcome and a deadline. The commitment may be an hour or a month. It might be created to attract one person who aches for a bit of meaning in their life.

We encourage a work crew boss to include at least two additional people on their crew: a person particularly skilled for the task at hand and an "outer orbit" person. This is someone the work crew boss invites to participate because we think they would enjoy pitching in on a short-term project.

Some work crews are permanent (events, financial durability, Team YL, Leader care). Most are more like flash mobs.

One last thing: we discourage the work crew boss from doing all the work on their own. We want expanding participation in the community God has created. We want Volunteers to grow through pitching in and experiencing spiritual enrichment.

This creates room for IMYL to grow. We want our town to experience growing community through common purpose.

8

DOES YOUR AREA LOSE TWO YEARS BECAUSE OF SUCCESSION?

And the things you have heard me say in the presence of many witnesses entrust to reliable people who will also be qualified to teach others.

—*2 Timothy 2:2*

For Intermountain Young Life, the idea of AD or CC succession isn't theoretical. We've experienced seamless successions of both Area Director and Committee Chair.

Andy's and my successful AD-CC relationship prepared the Area for leadership succession. Thanks to weekly meetings, both partners are up on the five major elements of the ministry:

- Spiritual Development
- Resource Development
- Ministry Support
- Leadership Development
- Direct Ministry

Andy got promoted and left our successful two-thousand-student ministry. He accepted an expanded AD role for fifteen thousand students in Seattle. For those of us still at IMYL, it was time for a transition.

Kaylan Riley had been serving with Andy on Staff since 2013. Previously, she was a Leader for five years and a Young Life kid.

She joined the Staff about a year after Andy and I repaired our relationship. She had seen what a strong AD-CC relationship looks like, how it works.

When we approached her about filling Andy's shoes as AD, she didn't hesitate.

Kaylan says, "I had seen the relationship modeled by Andy and Eric, and I didn't have any reservations. I stepped in as Area Director with a new baby. For women on Staff, lonesomeness can be even more. We're trying to play a role of mother, and we're trying to play a role of Area Director. I probably would not have stayed on Staff had it not been for a partnership. But with a strong AD-CC relationship, I knew it wouldn't be all on my shoulders. And thank God."

A couple of years passed. It was now 2020.

"Kaylan," I said during one of our weekly meetings, "I feel a prompting to retire as Committee Chair. What would you think?"

Kaylan raised her brows. Then she smiled. "We have a core value for this!"

She knew, personal feelings aside, one of our values is we don't hold on to anyone who feels their time has come to move into a new season. We celebrate them.

Then she added, "Eric, I will adjust, and I know God will find a replacement like He always has."

At the time, we were a few months into the pandemic. I pointed out, "We've been successful at reconfiguring Club, Campaigners, direct ministry, camp, and fund-raising. We are in good shape for going forward but not quite where we need to be for the best possible transition."

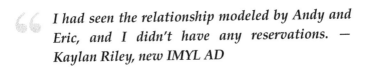

> *I had seen the relationship modeled by Andy and Eric, and I didn't have any reservations. —Kaylan Riley, new IMYL AD*

We dove into our fears. I'd recently done some work with Ken Tankersley and Kimberly Silvernale in the Global Innovation Department of YL regarding the key characteristics of a CC, so we had a good idea what to look for. We prayed and kept our eyes open for my replacement.

Here's what we sought:

- a faithful follower of Christ through prayer and action
- a gatherer of people
- someone who would treasure and nurture donor relationships
- someone willing to meet face-to-face weekly with the AD
- someone willing to attend monthly regional CC calls
- someone willing to uphold IMYL values

A few months later I got a giddy call from Kaylan.

"Eric! I've just had the most fantastic conversation over coffee with a woman who I think is our next Committee Chair."

I was confident in Kaylan. "How long has this person lived in Evergreen?" I asked.

"She doesn't live in the Area."

"She doesn't?"

"She lives fifteen miles away, but she's moving here in the next year."

She sounded like a good candidate. At first we tried to

keep our options open. But when God wants something, He can be kind of insistent at making it known.

Welcome Krista Wallace and her husband, Chad. Oh my, a chapter about their YL history is warranted, but in brief, they have been around YL all their lives. They have been on Staff; they have been Leaders, and they are praying lovers of kids and Christ.

And did I mention they were in the Dominican Republic for nineteen years, seven on YL Staff? This stood out to me. I remember thinking, *Imagine what perspective and experience they will bring, which I could not offer! Imagine how much will be new and inspiring!*

I felt the last of my concerns about leaving the CC job carried away on a cool mountain breeze.

After thirteen years in the ministry, many as Committee Chair, I retired from the role. God brought Krista and Chad Wallace to our town to serve our kids.

I had led our AD transition from Andy to Kaylan. Kaylan led the CC transition from me to Krista and Chad. And we didn't lose any time or momentum.

The AD-CC relationship *is* the silver bullet, and it proves itself in every weekly AD-CC meeting.

It proves itself in ministry to kids.

And it proves itself during transitions.

9

REFLECTIONS ON DEFINITIONS OF COMMUNITY

How good and pleasant it is when God's people live together in unity!

—*Psalm 133:1*

When I first took on the privilege and responsibility of CC for our Area, I had a goal. Ministry would be most desirable if we could create a successful community. I wanted community for myself. I wanted community for our town. And as Committee Chair, I welcomed the challenge. I thought to myself, *I'm the right guy for this job. Let's get this community started!*

Wow, did I get this one wrong.

Dietrich Bonhoeffer explained, "Christian community is not an ideal which we must realize."[1]

My first thought was, *Wait. What? Yes, it is attainable and I'm the guy to do it!*

But then I looked closer. There wasn't a period after the word *realize*—there was a semicolon. Bonhoeffer's thought wasn't completed. He went on to explain.

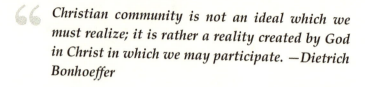

> *Christian community is not an ideal which we must realize; it is rather a reality created by God in Christ in which we may participate.* —*Dietrich Bonhoeffer*

The community is already there! Forehead slap. Don't create, *participate*!

I wasted years creating some pale version of community that got in the way of what God has already created in and for all of us. He not only designed each of us with a deep desire to be in community, but He also met this deep desire before it ever crossed our minds. We simply have to recognized what He has already created and join in!

The result? Andy and I submitted. We learned to take our hands off the wheel and just joyfully participate. We really did.

We started by converting three of our four annual events to celebrations of community. No ask, no fund-raising. We simply invited people to come with friends and family to celebrate the community God created for us because He loves us. Community grew and grew. People wanted this. They found meaning. They didn't feel leveraged or used. They felt welcome. Community was for them. It was for all of us.

> And let us consider how we may spur one another on toward love and good deeds, not giving up meeting together, as some are in the habit of doing, but encouraging one another—and all the more as you see the Day approaching. (Hebrews 10:24–25)

These days, I go to events like our annual Shrimp Boil. Fresh shrimp from the Louisiana coast to Colorado. All cooked to perfection. Hot shrimp dumped on long tables with butcher paper, corn, and potatoes. No chairs. No ask. No fee. We face each other over shrimp piled in the middle and create a holy mess.

It's famous and joyfully attended in our small mountain town.

My greatest joy is to meet someone I've never seen before. "I'm Virginia, and I've been working as a Volunteer for Wyld-Life for three years. You said your name is Eric? What do you do?"

I have no need for a descriptive answer. I'm not there as a Committee Chair or founder. I'm simply participating in the community God created for us. Participant is so much better. More of you, God. Less of me.

> *Christianity means community through Jesus Christ and in Jesus Christ. No Christian community is more or less than this.[2] —Dietrich Bonhoeffer*

I promise we are bold for Christ and kids for funding for our town and our kids in our annual banquet. Everyone expects an ask, and they give as they celebrate community there as well. At every event the community knows what to expect.

I have two community takeaways for you.

First, the AD-CC relationship fits like a dovetail joint with God's created community. It is such a load off our backs, such a reduction of our fears. Trusting ourselves created problems, but after seven tough years, it became easy to truly trust God.

Second, when it comes to the title of CC, I have come to prefer Community Chair over Committee Chair. The Area Director represents YL, and the Community Chair represents the community. The community and the YL organization have a profound common interest in pooling their unique knowledge.

One last thing. Promise me you'll read at least the first chapter of Bonhoeffer's book *Life Together*. You may not think it's necessary to make this extra effort, but it is. You'll gain a deep perspective on what life together can mean. As the Psalm says and Bonhoeffer repeats, "How good and pleasant it is when God's people live together in unity!" A rich community for your town, your kids, for yourself, and for your role in YL.

10

A BAKER'S DOZEN TAKEAWAYS

Consider it pure joy, my brothers and sisters, whenever you face trials of many kinds, because you know that the testing of your faith produces perseverance. Let perseverance finish its work so that you may be mature and complete, not lacking anything.

—James 1:2–4

1) BUILD ON PRAYER.

Trust God more than you trust yourselves. He provides. We pray as a community at 5:55 p.m. every evening.

2) WAGE WAR ON STAFF FEAR AND LONESOMENESS.

Fear and lonesomeness are not normal! But they are widespread and destructive. Ministry will remain stunted and fragile when leadership, or anyone in the ministry, is lonesome or afraid. Address this scourge through the AD-CC partnership. Intentionally identify and address fears.

3) CONSIDER AN "OUR TOWN, OUR KIDS" PERSPECTIVE AS YOUR PRIMARY ORGANIZING FOCUS.

"Our Town, Our Kids" has transformational meaning for your community. Young Life walking with our town. Man, it's fun when we are truly in this together.

4) DON'T OUTSOURCE YOUR KIDS' SALVATION.

Your town can't outsource your kids' salvation. You can try, but it won't work.

5) MODEL AD-CC LEADERSHIP THAT IS STRONG AND UNITED.

Your town will follow your example.

6) READ DIETRICH BONHOEFFER'S BOOK *LIFE TOGETHER*.

Read and share chapter 1. Your place in your YL Area will become clear.

7) OWN YOUR AREA.

Young Life fills part of the gap in kid ministry left vacant by your town, but it can only do so much. Be true partners. Accept ownership of your Area as soon as feasible. Own your Area, and your town will take responsibility for your town and your kids. Ownership will curtail outsourcing your kids' salvation, and blaming the AD will stop.

8) HONOR YOUNG LIFE.

Your town is blessed to have YL and YL Staff to walk with you. Love them as called ministers of the gospel. They are not employees.

9) BE INTENTIONAL ABOUT PROFESSIONAL DEVELOPMENT.

Develop the professional skills of your YL Staff so they can grow in capability. Grow them to serve the Lord and interact with your town. Support their careers and their movement. Don't cling to them.

10) THE YL AREA IS PART OF THE CHURCH.

Each YL Area is an organism that is fully part of the church and integrated with the faith community of your town. Some may see the YL Area as separate or parallel. Make sure it isn't.

11) PURSUE HEALTH AND GROWTH.

Chapter 7, "Our Approach for a Healthy YL Area," provides a template that works. Try it, then make improvements that make it more effective for your Area.

12) UTILIZE THE SUM OF THE PARTS.

Your town and your kids will flourish when you integrate the wisdom of your town and the expertise of YL. Become one in the body of Christ.

13) REMEMBER THAT JESUS IS "THE BREAD OF LIFE" (JOHN 6:35).

The Pharisees exhausted themselves with overcommitment and the illusion of what control offers. Andy and I exhausted ourselves and each other too. We tried to speed up. Turns out we needed to slow down.

The world is lost and longing for connection.

Jesus offered *ridiculous inefficiency* in relationships. Time well wasted is incomprehensible to today's citizen. This gives you an opportunity to offer a unique gift to your town.

Your AD-CC leadership can transform your town and your kids. You've been entrusted. And in the end Andy and I pray you hear, "Well done, good and faithful servant! . . . Come and share your master's happiness!" (Matthew 25:23).

11

I'M INTERESTED. WHERE CAN I START?

Whatever you do, work at it with all your heart, as working for the Lord, not for human masters, since you know that you will receive an inheritance from the Lord as a reward. It is the Lord Christ you are serving.

—Colossians 3:23–24

It has been our desire to share our story, and we've sought to avoid telling you what to do. However, you may have become attracted to something in our story you'd like to pursue.

At the end of this chapter, you'll find Gill Richard's "A Prayer for Our Town." Pray it over yourself, your Area, and your town. Does it speak to you or to your personal ministry?

I'M INTERESTED. WHERE DO I START?

Does your heart ache for a better YL Area?

If the AD-CC relationship Andy and I developed sounds

good to you, this doesn't mean everyone with a stake is equally interested.

Don't surprise any stakeholder.

Consider your current Area Director—maybe that's you. Consider your current Committee Chair—again, maybe that's you. They don't have to participate in the reimagined relationship. Perhaps you're meeting once a month, fifteen minutes before the Committee meeting. This may be what current stakeholders are comfortable with. Maybe this is all you or they wish to do. Explore, but recognize and honor this about them.

This kind of AD-CC relationship is happening now in a lot of places in the mission. But it is not typical. It is likely none of your stakeholders are familiar with this arrangement. Share this book with them, and let it do the work. Let Andy's and my story be evaluated. Then share your thoughts. Give everyone a chance to thoughtfully respond.

If the conversations go well, remember that a strong partnership takes time to develop. Earn the right to be heard. Build a deep relationship based on godly trust.

Identify each stakeholder's expectations. Write them down, compare, then align. Have the conversations.

In the meantime, if you have questions, you're welcome to reach out to Kaylan, to me, or to Andy. We can surely save you some heartache and time.

GILL RICHARD'S "A PRAYER FOR OUR TOWN"

When God was just starting to heal Andy's and my relationship and show us a better way, the following prayer was spoken over me and other CCs. It encouraged me greatly, and I hope it encourages you as well.

My friend for life Gill Richard is the Front Range Regional Board Chairman for another friend for life, RD Terry Leprino.

Gill runs a monthly gathering for Committee Chairs. It is such a blessing. He has seen my travails. He has seen my story.

One day as Andy and I were just starting to figure things out, Gill asked me a question just before a monthly regional CC gathering:

"Eric, how are things in Intermountain Young Life?"

"Fabulous."

"No, really?"

"Well, Gill, you know it has been up and down. We've learned a lot, and we probably talk like we've got it all figured out. It is good, but nothing is all smooth."

Gill addressed the gathering. "To all of you serving as CCs, I'd like to pray for you."

I transcribed his wise and insightful prayer. I've included it here, and I hope it encourages you as much as it encouraged me.

A PRAYER FOR OUR TOWN

Lord, is this our town and are these kids our kids?
What do you Lord ask of our town?
Lord, are we in any way outsourcing our kids' salvation when we shouldn't? Is outsourcing something we truly can't do even if we want to? Is this something we truly can't do even if we feel encouraged to do so?
Lord, what role does Young Life play in our town?
Lord, would you guide us in discernment for what is right and wrong in how we are approaching our town and our kids?
Lord, are we overestimating what an Area Director can do, and are we headed for preventable disappointment and pain?
Lord, protect us from any missteps and guide us to the clarity of your expectations.
Lord, show us how to balance the responsibilities you've given us as parents and leaders with the strengths and potential of Young Life.
Lord, we love our town and our kids. We newly recognize and appreciate these children are our responsibility, always and forever, awarded by you. We are grateful for Young Life. We appreciate the tools, traditions, and know-how Young Life has contributed.
The assistance we get from Young Life and not the assistance we provide to Young Life is how we fulfill what you've assigned us.
Amen.

APPENDIX

REAL TALK, AN AD-CC REGIONAL VIDEO LINK AND TRANSCRIPT

This is a transcript of a conversation held by Area Directors and Staff during a Heartland Regional Zoom meeting on December 17, 2020.

This transcript has been edited to correct minor errors and to highlight the topics found in this book. You may listen to the REAL TALK conversation at:

ericprotzmanauthor.com

Participants on the call:

- Mark Sisler – Moderator, Regional Initiatives Coordinator, Heartland Region 2019–present
- Andy Morman – IMYL Area Director 2008–2017
- Eric Protzman – IMYL Committee Chair 2008–2009, 2014–2020
- Kaylan Riley – IMYL Area Director 2017–present
- Krista & Chad Wallace – IMYL Committee Chair 2020–present

MARK SISLER

Welcome, Heartland Region, to our special Zoom session from around the country. All about the relationship between the Area Director and the Committee Chair. We've got a lot of stuff to go over. Hopefully a lot of this stuff will be just a great way for you to listen and engage on topics with your Committee Chair that we're going to be talking about today. So, I'd like to introduce everybody and have a chance for them to kind of share what their piece of the puzzle is today. And kind of where their perspective is going to come from in regards to what they're going to be sharing. So why don't we go ahead and start in the upper left-hand corner of my screen with Eric. So go ahead, Eric.

Eric Protzman

I'm Eric Protzman. I live in Evergreen, Colorado. I've been involved with Young Life since I came to faith in high school. I've been involved for twenty-five years, and Nancy and I started Young Life here in Evergreen in 2007. I've been Committee Chair twice, just most recently retiring about ten days ago.

Mark Sisler

Krista, why don't you go next.

Krista Wallace

Okay, so I'm Krista Wallace, the new Committee Chair. My husband and I live in Evergreen. We were on Staff with Young Life for seven years. I've been involved for thirty-five years since I was fourteen.

Chad Wallace

So same kind of story. Was involved in Young Life as a high school student and a Volunteer Leader in high school and then took a hiatus in college when I was involved in some other ministries. My wife got plugged back in with Young Life. We were on Staff in the Dominican Republic for those seven years. On Committee and Volunteer Leader since then. So, we've never really cut those ties.

Mark Sisler

Right, Andy?

ANDY MORMAN

Yeah, my name is Andy Morman. I was on Staff in Evergreen, Colorado, for about nine years. I'm just about ready to complete my fifteenth year on Staff, currently an Area Director on the east side of Seattle, and have had the privilege of knowing Eric and Kaylan for a lot of years. A Young Life kid since high school. I'm married and have three kids. We're loving this season of our lives.

MARK SISLER

Kaylan, what about you?

KAYLAN RILEY

Hey, my name is Kaylan Riley. I am the current Area Director of Intermountain Young Life in Evergreen, Colorado. And I started with Young Life in high school. I was a Young Life kid my sophomore year and was a Volunteer Leader for five years. I went on Staff under Andy when he was Area Director in Evergreen in 2013. I became the Area Director in 2017. So, I'm the current Area Director of Intermountain Young Life.

MARK SISLER

Right. Thank you for all the introductions. We'll start with Andy. Andy, you served both in Colorado and now in Washington. As you think of your experiences with the Committee, with two different Committees, what are your observations? What would you share with Area Directors as far as the things that you've been a part of? Things you've seen.

ANDY MORMAN

Yeah. It's been interesting to be a part of a lot of these Committee conversations. I've experienced kind of the nonexistent Committee model where I'm like, apparently we have a Committee, but I've never seen them. That was my first couple years on Staff. I've been told we have a Committee, but I'm not sure what their role is in my life and how they affect my life. There's been times where I've experienced the whole "Hey,

Area Director, we need you to do these things, we expect you to do these things, and why aren't you doing these things?" I've experienced the weight of that. I've also experienced the beautiful other side where I feel like I have a team of people who are with me and who are arm in arm together on a mission for the sake of kids in Christ. And so, a lot of it's been joyful. A lot of it's been really hard. I empathize with a lot of the Staff in the room. And the Staff that I've come in contact with where, you know, there's an experience of being lonely and afraid in our mission that I think is epidemic. And I think that, gosh, sometimes the Committee and Committee Chair relationship can be the cause of that fear and lonesomeness. And but I also think it's the cure. And I've experienced that as well. I've experienced a wide variety of different kind of Committee setups and experiences. But I've loved some of the realizations we've had over the last five or six years in terms of oh, like, this is one of the most important parts of our mission. When we get it right, big things happen. So, I'm excited to have this conversation today.

MARK SISLER

Okay, Eric, same question for you, what have you seen, what are observations you've seen in the realm of Committee?

ERIC PROTZMAN

I've seen it in three stages, Mark. I've observed, participated in, to my shame, the "hire the Area Director and blame them" model. Young Life can show up sometimes a little over-confident or a little over representing what they're going to do. And it can make it seem like they're going to take on everything and do it, and that they don't really need help. And then it kind of turns around, they start asking for help. And you get a dynamic going on the first of the three phases that I've seen, that either the Area Director or the Committee Chair or both come in with sort of a "you owe me" attitude. The Area Director may come in and say, "I could have been a stockbroker, I could have made this money, I could have done this, but instead, I'm here in your town. This town owes me because I do these things." And you can have a Committee Chair saying, "Hey, we hired you, we raised the money for you here, you owe us." It's just a terrible dynamic. And if any Area Directors are listening to that or there are any Committee Chairs listening, then search your heart for that one, because nothing will work if you hold that "you owe me" view as an Area Director or as Committee Chair.

The second phase came with the realization Committee was a blessing from our Lord to Andy and to me. Sometimes you want a businessperson Committee Chair, so I'm kind of that person. I came in viewing the Area Director role as a vocational role. And I addressed Andy as having a job and with the job had expectations. And this should be done by this time, and so on. And it didn't work out very well for either of us. And the Lord spoke to me, and he spoke to Andy. To me, it was, "Look, you've been kind of hard on this guy, and you are a person that loves people. Get in there and love him and I'll get back to you." And I moved from viewing the Area Director position as a vocational role into a ministry role. Ministers need to minister, and they need to be ministered to. That really shifted everything.

Then the third level, where Andy and I, led by the Lord, figured out, we're in this together. There are no problems that are Andy's or are mine. Every problem is ours. If Andy says, we've got a problem and I've caused it, Andy and I must solve it. If there's a problem and Andy caused it, Andy and I must solve it. If there's another problem and Mark Sisler in Iowa has caused it, Andy and I still must solve it. That's it. That was the third level. And that's when things got good.

Mark Sisler

Andy, as you transitioned from Colorado to Washington, tell us a little bit about the role of the Committee and the Committee Chair in that transition.

Andy Morman

Eric and I had been on this journey. Well, there's a longer story that we'd love to show you someday, but where we began our relationship . . . Eric was responsible for hiring me. And we began our relationship just in love with each other. Greatest friends soon became our greatest enemies and hated each other. And then the Lord somehow did some work, some magic, where not only I love Eric, but my wife loves Eric, which that is a whole other miracle. A long road back, baby. If that's not a teaser, I don't know what is. I had experienced something with Eric in terms of partnership that in transition into a new role, where I would be with a new Committee, and a new Committee Chair, there's some non-negotiable things for me. I've experienced what it means to be in partnership with a Committee Chair, to do this thing with somebody else, arm in arm. I'm just not willing to go back to the island that I think that a lot of our Staff, myself included, were wrong in terms of that lonely and afraid place. I just wasn't going to last on Staff. And so, from the very beginning—and thankfully, our new Committee Chair, Taylor, was able to hear Eric's and my story and kind of what we've been through. And it turns out that Taylor had always been hungry for that type of a role. He didn't want to be a helper; he wanted to be someone who was a partner and someone who was in it, hands dirty, with an Area Director. He was told that he was supposed to be someone who cheered me on. I think he was thankful from the very beginning of our relationship to know, "No, this is gonna be different, like, we're accountable to each other." We are here for each other, we're available to each other, we're in this together, we're indivisible. You're my partner, you're not less than. And it's been a gift to me walking into a new relationship to have that as the backbone. I mean, I had a conversation before I got on this call that was heavy, and it was hard. Someone was disappointed with some stuff that was going on in our Area, and I left it carefree. I know that I have a Committee Chair who's with me, that if there are things we need to fix, he and I will do it together. But that conversation, six years ago, would have destroyed me. I'd be out for a few days, feeling horrible. To walk out of a hard conversation and to feel like I can take on those barriers and those difficulties is a gift.

I know a lot of our Staff don't feel that. And so that's why we're so passionate about this story of partnership and connection.

MARK SISLER

So, did prayer play a role in your relationship with Eric, changing from where you say it wasn't very good to where it became a friendship?

ANDY MORMAN

Man, I mean, again, there's a longer story. But there were Eric and I, as the Lord was working on us, and it was difficult. There was some significant disappointment where I disappointed Eric and Eric disappointed me. There was a lot of pain and hurt. And I think for both of us. The word that is Eric's and my least favorite word is assumptions. I think we realized that the enemy had used assumptions we'd made about each other in terms of our motivations, in terms of why we chose to do things, and in terms of what Eric thought about me. I had countless conversations with Eric that I never actually had with him. As I was going to bed stressing out, I was having conversations with Eric that, again, were just made up. They weren't real. And there was one day I remember I was mopping my floor in my house. My wife was putting the kids to bed. And I think I was listening to something on my headphones or whatever. And I just was overwhelmed. I was having to endure this painful conversation. I was having this conversation with imaginary Eric, and I asked the Lord. I was like, *Lord, this isn't of you. Would you please, would you please end this dialogue?* And it ended, and I went to the restroom, closed the door, and I called Eric, and I was like, "Eric, I just I'm so sorry. And I know I've hurt you." But I just, yeah, it was just

. . . it just . . . I'm remembering what I said. But it was one of those things where I was like, hey, I'm just done carrying this burden. And just to watch as the Lord redeem things from that space was incredible. And something Eric and I look back on even today. I'm just like, man, we were in a hard spot.

ERIC PROTZMAN

If it had been up to Andy and me, we probably wouldn't be speaking. We would not care about each other or for each other. And this is one of my best friends on the planet here. So, the answer to your question, Mark, on prayer, was the Lord answered prayer spoken and unspoken, that he had dreams for this Area. And he was going to get them done. And it was either going to happen in this go round or some future go round. I don't care what anybody thinks about what I think about how God worked on us. This is my story. This is Andy's story. You couldn't take this away from us. Because it wasn't me.

ANDY MORMAN

We're not that good. But God is really good. Yeah.

MARK SISLER

Kaylan, as you transitioned to the Area Director when Andy left for Washington, tell us about the role of the Committee Chair. Obviously, that was Eric who just shared with us. Did you have any trepidation at that point in time? Things had gotten better between Andy and Eric. So, were there any thoughts on your part, you know, as far as how that was gonna go? Share with us your thoughts.

KAYLAN RILEY

Yeah. So, I stepped into my role about a year after Andy and Eric had repaired their relationship. So, I had seen it modeled really well. I really didn't have any reservations about it. I actually didn't know the full story of Eric and Andy. And I think that, that was a blessing and something that I learned as I've been in my role now but didn't know it in the beginning. I was in a unique spot. When I became Area Director, three weeks later I went on maternity leave. So sorry about that. And my husband was in school. So we were a single-income family. And I stepped into being Area Director with a new baby. And for women on Staff, I feel like the lonesome-ness is, can be, even more, because we're trying to play a role of mother and we're trying to play a role of Area Director, and yeah, I stepped in a place that really needed a partnership. And I don't think I would have survived, I mean, the first few months that I was on Staff. We had some really hard things happen in our Area. And I can honestly say, I probably would have not stayed on Staff had it not been for a partnership. Going to bed every night knowing that it wasn't just me, this wasn't all on my shoulders. And thank God for that. Because now, what, a little over three years later, I'm still here. And I don't see an end in sight. And I have another kid and a new Committee Chair and a friendship with Eric. And now I have a friendship with Krista that's really sweet.

MARK SISLER

How did you develop that feeling of partnership between you and Eric?

KAYLAN RILEY

You know, honestly, we said it a lot, and we would say over and over again, like, you're my partner, we are in this together. And sometimes it can feel really cheesy, like, we're partners. But that is the truth. And I think that when we speak that over and over again, it really becomes true on our hearts. And there are so many times that something would happen and I would call Eric, or he would call me, and we'd just remind each other, "Hey, we got this together." And the weight that, that would take off was huge. In a time where sleepless nights were already a lot, I didn't need any more of those. So yeah, honestly, just saying it over and over again, this is my partner, we're in this together, and reminding yourself, like, we've already said that we're not just here for Young Life. We're here for Jesus and for kids, our town, and our kids meeting the God of the universe. And to come back to that often to remind yourself that as partners, that's our focus.

MARK SISLER

Krista and Chad, what do you guys have as far as thoughts on this topic so far?

CHAD WALLACE

We need to feel cared for and we need to be in community. I think one of the things that people are drawn to Young Life is because it's a fun community where you feel known, and especially for kids, but as adults and Young Life Staff and Committee, we uncomplicate that relationship. I think what you said, Kaylan, about speaking it—it's truth and it becomes a reality. Thank you, Eric, for doing that. I do sense that from you. You do speak the same thing over and over and eventually believe it. Really, thank you for that.

KRISTA WALLACE

I mean, this is a team effort. It's not my responsibility, it's not Eric's, it's not Kaylan's, it is ours, right? We encourage one another as teammates.

MARK SISLER

What would you say to an Area Director and a Committee Chair that are watching this that maybe aren't in that partnership relationship right now? They're in the stage where they want the other person to do more or the Area Director doesn't feel supported. How would they go about bringing the change that you guys experienced into their Area?

ERIC PROTZMAN

The first thing is, don't approach me and ask me to support Young Life. Don't approach me and ask me to support you. That puts me on a different level. It discounts me. It elevates you. As you invite me, you have to presume that I already care about the kids in my town. Rather say, "You know what, there are a lot of kids at that school. I think I can really help this community get to those kids. Yeah, Eric, how can I work with you so we can really reach those kids." There is a world of difference. Anybody listening here. If you invite people to support Young Life, that's tiny. I refuse to support Young Life. I love Young Life, I came to faith in Young Life, but I can't allow that posture. Young Life is not my purpose. We're here for our town, our kids. You want to join me in that, you're going to get a volcano of partnership.

ANDY MORMAN

Maybe even a step before what Eric just shared, this idea Eric and I talked a lot about aligning expectations. You're at the beginning stages of that relationship with a Committee Chair that, you know, maybe it might be a lukewarm relationship, maybe it's somewhat problematic. Sit down with your Committee Chair and make a list of what you're expecting of the Committee Chair. And for them to do the same thing for the Area Director. And just be able to share and put it on the table. I just want to make sure that we are clear on our expectations of each other. And I think that more often than not, what we've seen, and a lot of what Eric and I struggled with, is that we were on totally different planets in our expectations for each other.

And honestly, for a lot of Committee Chairs and Area Directors, that has been the avenue in which they start to talk about partnership when they can get those things out of the way. Even in a scenario like with Krista and Kaylan, for them to begin their relationship, get your expectations on the table. It just removes all the stuff that eventually is gonna be land mines that they step on down the road. So, I think that it's a healthy practice for any Area Director–Committee Chair relationship, however good or bad their relationship is, because eventually you're going to start to automatically identify like, oh man, like, I am really disappointed right now. Because I've assumed that so-and-so is going to do this, and they haven't. If you're really honest, have you even communicated that to them, or have you just assumed it? So, those things are major land mines that can destroy relationships and partnerships.

MARK SISLER

Andy, why don't you share a little bit about what you'd say to an Area Director who thinks, you know, I'm not sure the Committee's really the way to go? It just, it seems burdensome. It seems like too much work. I'm not sure it's worth the effort. How would you respond to somebody who maybe is in that situation and in that mind-set?

ANDY MORMAN

I would say this as an Area Director. I look at Committees and adult work and adult support as really like my legacy. Like, how well do I work with adults and in partnership with my community will be my legacy in my Area. You know, Eric and I talk a lot about how the most consistent thing in our town is our community. Staff come and go; Leaders come and go.

Community is going to remain for the long term. That's the reason why we invest in adults. As a Staff person, you can't do it on your own. If you're a young Staff person, and you think that you can do it, you think you've got to figure it out. It serves you well to realize that you don't have it figured out and that's okay; you have a community of people, you have adults in your life who want to do this with you. And actually, let's be honest, they know more than you. They have more life experience. And so, the more we can elevate those around us in partnership, and to do this with them, the better legacy you're going to have in an Area. And the less of a negative impact you are leaving someday is going to have. The community will get better as a result. I want to leave anywhere that I'm at to where it's going to catapult after I leave. I think the only way you can do that is through investing in your adult community.

MARK SISLER

So, Eric, how do you structure your weekly meetings? You've done this with a couple different Staff people over a number of years? One of the things we've talked about is how important it is for that Area Director and the Committee Chair to meet on a weekly basis face-to-face. What does that look like?

ERIC PROTZMAN

Well, Andy and I came up with a format that that's been used in Intermountain Young Life for six years. We believe in prayer; prayer saved our relationship, so we start with prayer. We know what the Lord has done for us. We're not about to leave Him now. Secondly, I ask Andy, "What are you afraid of?" And now, the new updated version and Kaylan looks at me and says Eric, "What are you afraid of?" And that is not limited to direct ministry. It's not limited to ministry in general. And we just believe profoundly you can't do ministry if you're afraid. Address fears honestly and lonesomeness virtually evaporates. If you're feeling lonesome, you call your Committee Chairs and things get better. But to have the sense of fear over work or over personal things, you've got to get it out there. What's the first agenda item beyond that? Our fears we just confessed. There's no point to not addressing the fears together. If you're afraid you're not going to meet the monthly budget, or if you're unexpectedly short on Leaders, there's no way you can just happily go about the rest of your day. You've got to address those things. I would say, most of the time, our meetings are just, "How are we figuring this out? I don't want you afraid, partner. I don't want you afraid." And they've helped me figure stuff out. I've helped them figure it out. Mostly, we've either figured it out together or we've looked at each other and admitted neither one of us has any idea how to do this. Well, we know somebody, and we can go ask them. So that's the way we structure it. And I'll tell you what, it is one of the most pleasing things that I've been around, the prayer and being honest about your fears. It took us a year to really start building trust, where we could love each other and just think good things. And we'd ask each other what we were afraid of, and Andy's answer eventually and usually became, "Nothing. I'm not afraid of anything."

ANDY MORMAN

Yes, the answer eventually became "nothing." You asked me that question every week and I am surprised by it now. Like I have no answer for it. I'd love to hear you, Kaylan. You walk into that system as a new Area Director of being asked about your fears, which is a pretty intimate question. That takes some vulnerability to talk about what you're afraid of, a lot of trust. What was that like for you to walk into that?

KAYLAN RILEY

It was honestly really helpful. Because it wasn't like one of us . . . it wasn't just ministry related. It was family related. It was anything-under-the-moon related. It was genuinely just what my fears are. And that makes it so much more of a relationship. And like you're saying, Chad, like, we just care about each other, and we have a relationship, and so why would you not ask that question? And it's true. It's fun to go to meetings where you were, like, not really afraid of anything. Great. And so sweet to vocalize that, and to feel that freedom with your partner, and then be able to look at them and see what their fears are, and they could be different, and you jump into them together.

ERIC PROTZMAN

I'd like to make a distinction to when you get to the point of no fears. That's not like it's easygoing. There's still a ton of work to do. But your fears in the past were how are you going to fix it when you didn't even know how to do it. You didn't have anybody to share it with. So, you were fearful of the work. But it is the lonesomeness that weighs you down. Not the work. Young Life people are not afraid of work. But we all get afraid if we feel alone and we don't know where to start. We will look at each other after saying we gotta roll up our sleeves, because we've got a lot to do.

KAYLAN RILEY

I think that was a . . . that's a good clarification of, there's a lot of times that it was, like, oh, gosh, yeah, we have a lot to do right now. But I'm not fearful of it. Because I know I can do the work. So yeah.

MARK SISLER

Our people, we had questions like, how do we help the Committee ask for financial support without feeling awkward? What does it mean to join Committee and share the ownership of the ministry for the long run? How do I get my Committee to take ownership? How does an individual member get involved in the Committee if there's no good or bad culture? And we kind of said that part of that is maybe a symptom of a larger problem. Andy, what would you say to these questions, and how would you look to build on this?

ANDY MORMAN

This is going to sound like an oversimplified answer, but it is absolutely the core of the answer, to all of those questions. When that Committee Chair relationship along with the Area Director is established, when there is a cohesive unit between the Area Director and Committee Chair, the Committee becomes more productive, and the adult community feels like they have something to follow, like a rally point. Funding happens, because you have multiple people who are thinking through it and trying to figure out what it looks like. It's not just the Area Director trying to solve different problems that have a scarcity mind-set. There's no one-thing-fixes-all except for the one thing that you are in control of as a Staff person, which is that Committee Chair relationship. And so, I think you start there, and then you figure out all of those answers together. Those are questions you ask in partnership, and you solve in partnership. And so, again, we overcomplicate the problems and we overcomplicate the relationship. It's a relationship where we get to solve hard problems together and to have disagreements together. And we get to the other side of those disagreements and move in a solid single direction together. So, don't get bogged down in an issue, focus on the relationship.

ERIC PROTZMAN

I suppose that we find young Area Directors are really comfortable working with kids but get freaked out working with adults. But work on that, Area Directors, because your very finest skill is creating relationships. And we're here with our arms open. We're not here to fight you. If you ask us just to help, it just gives us small-potatoes stuff to do. Yeah, we're going to look pretty uninterested. But we're the people that started the soccer teams. We're the ones that built the bank, and we're the ones that built the town. Okay, we know how to do stuff. And if you're thinking we're running away and irresponsible, think hard about how relationships get built with kids. Use those skills that you have. We want to be loved just like you. I promise you. I'm an eight-year-old boy. I want to be loved. I am not needy. I'm not desperate. I am a child of God and I want to be loved. Don't treat me different than a kid because I am a kid.

MARK SISLER

So, pursuing the adult on the Committee, whether it be the, you know, the Committee Chair or just someone that's on the Committee, pursuing them the way that you might, as an Area Director, pursue students. Getting to know them, showing up where they are. Investing in that relationship and just kind of wasting time together is so important on the adult level, is kind of what I'm hearing, right?

ERIC PROTZMAN

No different.

KRISTA WALLACE

Yeah. And I would even go further, even beyond Committee, you know, the principals and the coaches at the school. I mean, you pursue adults, the same adults that are involved in our kids' lives.

MARK SISLER

Now, it's good, that's good. What do you look for in a Committee Chair? We have some people out there in the process of looking for a new Committee Chair. You start praying about, you know, Lord, who would you bring next? What are we looking for as we think of a Committee Chair?

ERIC PROTZMAN

I told Kaylan, last February, I think that I'd like to look at a transition. And I'd like to look at it by the end of the year. So, it was eight to ten months. And we set about putting together a list of what we thought would constitute a successful Committee Chair. First thing is a follower of Christ. And as obvious as that might be, you can get the PTA president from last year that really did a good job, but goes to church and is thinking, "Maybe I'll take a crack at leading this one." You know what I'm saying? You want somebody who is a faithful, day-in-day-out follower of Christ first. That's immutable. Secondly, you need a connector. You need somebody who can't help but connect people together. That's what they love to do. That's what they want to do. You can't stop them from doing it. If you don't have that, it's tough. They don't create community; God creates community, and we get to participate in it. But the connector plays a really important role. They must prize and be able to nurture relationships including donor relationships. For us, they had to agree to meet face-to-face weekly with the Area Director. You can tell from this video why we all believe in it so much, so meet face-to-face weekly. If it's Zoom, it's still face-to-face. Our region offers regional Committee Chair meetings, and we said attendance would be a good requirement. And then they have to, at least initially, agree to our core values that we've got written down. These are the things that we really think are important, because if you don't agree with those, it's going to be tough. Our culture is built on our core values. And so, that's where we are as we looked for a Committee Chair, and we succeeded.

MARK SISLER

Do you think it's hard to find somebody that would fulfill those characteristics?

ERIC PROTZMAN

There are a couple of you Area Directors watching who are saying, "This would be easy if I had that row of people that I'm seeing here on Zoom. That'd be just fine. Why don't you pack up and move to my town? Then everything will be fine." Okay, I want to promise you, we exist in every community. You won't find us if you just ask us to support Young Life or if you ask us to just be your helper. We love our town and our kids and we want them to meet Jesus. Joining us in that encourages us. You can bring so much. But the first thing Area Directors who are saying, "How in the world do I find those people?" I say, just go find a friend. Just find a friend that might not be your Committee Chair. But I'll tell you my experience about 50 percent of the time it ends up God puts people together. But go find a friend, somebody you can create a relationship with, and say, "Will you just walk with me for the next six months?" I need intense prayer. I need somebody to meet with every month. "I am not trying to recruit you as a Committee Chair. I'm gonna be looking for one at some point. Maybe you'll find one for me." But your next joy in ministry is gonna start with that one relationship. One friend and it's gonna start with your heart in the right spot.

ANDY MORMAN

Krista, what was it like for you to walk into this role, one that is elevated and had some clarity attached to it? You actually know what you're getting yourself into. My assumption is you're like, "Oh, I would love to be a partner rather than a helper." Right?

KRISTA WALLACE

Yes. So, when I first met Kaylan, which was about six months ago, we knew we were moving to Evergreen. And there was just this really cool connection. I think because I had been praying about what I want, I mean, just being prayerful about this whole scenario. And I'm assuming, I'm going to say that Kaylan was prayerful as well. We came together at just this God-oriented time. We met for about an hour. When I walked out of there, I was on cloud nine.

KAYLAN RILEY

I was like, I have a new friend.

KRISTA WALLACE

We need to be prayerful about it. It's not just a community service, right? I know that this is a calling. I want to say yes to God's calling. So, let's be prayerful, both in seeking and in finding and nurturing that relationship.

MARK SISLER

As we think about this weekly meeting between the Committee Chair and the Area Director, how does this work?

KAYLAN RILEY

We start off talking about our fears. And a lot of our agenda typically can roll out of that. You may be thinking that feels very, like, you're just trying to combat whatever's happening in that moment. But that's not true at all. We also have an agenda that we both put stuff into, over the week. It's already happened with Krista, which is not surprising.

ERIC PROTZMAN

We've agreed on the top priorities, the top one, the second, and the next. We build our agenda around those priorities, and if they don't fit in those priorities, we pretty much don't do them.

MARK SISLER

As we kind of look to wrap things up, what are the two most important things you can think of that, you know, someone could do starting today?

ERIC PROTZMAN

I think "don't shock anybody." This AD-CC relationship is being done. What we're talking about is happening now in a lot of places in the mission. But it is not typical. Don't shock your supervisor. Let them know what your thoughts are on this. And don't shock your current Committee Chair. They didn't sign up for this. Give them a chance to respond. They don't have to become this. If this relationship sounds good to you, that doesn't mean that person's gonna change overnight. If you're meeting once a month, fifteen minutes before the Committee meeting, that's what they're comfortable with. Maybe that's all they want to do. Recognize and honor that. But have the conversations. And you're welcome to reach out to Kaylan, to me, to Andy. I'd start with a conversation with your supervisor; then I'd start a conversation with your Committee Chair. Get your heart right before you go into any of those things.

ANDY MORMAN

Yeah, if your Committee Chair has willingness to sit down, then do that exercise of "here's what I expect of our Committee Chair," and have them do the same thing with their expectations of you as Area Director. For Eric and myself, it took us a year of—and this will be true for you, Krista—we just have to call each other partners almost to where we laugh about it.

MARK SISLER

That's great. Is there anything that anybody wants to share that you're like, hey, we really need to talk about this, that we haven't talked about this topic?

ERIC PROTZMAN

Right. And my hat is off to Andy Morman. This Area is thriving. We have a new Committee Chair with a worldview and a different way of looking at things and that is going to add to this. People have called me and said, "What? Really? What's the deal? Why are you leaving?" It's like, are you kidding me? I'm leaving because I'm proud of where it is. It is strong, financially strong, spiritually strong, and strong in direct ministry. It's a perfect time to step away. I couldn't be happier. I couldn't be more grateful for what being involved with IMYL has done for my life, my friendships, and all I've learned. It's a lot of work, but it's a joy.

MARK SISLER

Good. All right. Well, thanks so much for all the things that we have learned that you've shared. Certainly grateful for the time each of you was willing to give, and hopefully this is something that can be used outside of our region and can be used in other places.

KAYLAN RILEY

Let me pray for all of us . . .

RECOMMENDED READING

For general insight:
Bonhoeffer, Dietrich Bonhoeffer. *Life Together: A Discussion of Christian Fellowship*. San Francisco: HarperCollins, 1954.
de Cassade, Jean-Pierre. *Abandonment to Divine Providence.* Trans. John Beevers. New York: Doubleday, 1975.
Manning, Brennan. *The Furious Longing of God.* Colorado Springs, CO: David C. Cook, 2009.
Mitchell, Bob. *Letters to a Young Life Leader.* Houston, TX: Whitecaps Media, 2012.
Senyard, Dr William H., *Fair Forgiveness: Finding the Power to Forgive Where You Least Expect It,* 2014.

For guidance on operations:
Grenny, Joseph, Kerry Patterson, Ron McMillan, Al Switzler, and Emily Gregoy. *Crucial Conversations: Tools for Talking When Stakes Are High.* Third ed. New York: McGraw Hill, 2022.
Wiseman, Liz. *Multipliers: How the Best Leaders Make Everyone Smarter.* New York: Harper Business, 2010.

NOTES

1. ARE YOU SETTING YOURSELF UP FOR DISAPPOINTMENT IN THE FIRST TEN MINUTES?

1. Young Life Committee Chair Handbook, revised March 2021, 12.
2. Young Life Committee Handbook, revised March 2021, 12. Also, Young Life Committee Chair Handbook revised June 2020, 12.

2. ARE YOU OUTSOURCING YOUR KIDS' SALVATION?

1. Every translation of Ephesians 6:4 ascribes instruction about the Lord as a parental responsibility.

3. ARE YOU APPROACHING YOUR YL AREA LIKE A BUSINESS?

1. Dietrich Bonhoeffer, *Life Together: The Classic Exploration of Christian Community* (San Francisco: Harper & Row, 1954), 30.

5. ARE YOU RECOGNIZING THE MOST IMPORTANT RELATIONSHIP IN THE AREA?

1. Ken "Tank" Tankersley, "A Ted Talk to Remember: My Last Conversation with Ted Johnson," The Young Life Leader Blog by Drew Hill, YoungLifeLeaders.org, April 5, 2021, https://younglifeleaders.org/2021/04/a-ted-talk-to-remember-my-last-conversation-with-ted-johnson.html.

6. ARE YOU INVITING VOLUNTEERS TO JOIN A STORY?

1. "A Christian College in Kentucky Has Experienced a Religious Awakening, *The Economist*, February 23, 2023, https://www.economist.-

com/united-states/2023/02/23/a-christian-college-in-kentucky-has-experienced-a-religious-awakening.

7. ARE YOU INTERESTED IN OUR APPROACH TO A HEALTHY AREA?

1. Joseph Grenny, Kerry Patterson, Ron McMillan, Al Switzler, and Emily Gregory, *Crucial Conversations: Tools for Talking When Stakes Are High*, 3rd ed. (New York: McGraw Hill, 2022).

9. REFLECTIONS ON DEFINITIONS OF COMMUNITY

1. Dietrich Bonhoeffer, *Life Together: A Discussion of Christian Fellowship* (San Francisco: HarperCollins, 1954), 30.
2. Dietrich Bonhoeffer, *Life Together*, 21.

ACKNOWLEDGMENTS

Thank you, Young Life! You've changed my life, and you've changed the world.

But blessed is the one who trusts in the LORD, whose confidence is in him. (Jeremiah 17:7)

I can do all this through him who gives me strength. (Philippians 4:13)

There are hundreds of adults and kids to thank. But since I'm aware the acknowledgments shouldn't be as long as the book, I've done my best to honor the remarkable IMYL community and others while staying brief.

And those of you whom I never would have knowingly left out. You know I love you.

Therefore, I'm recognizing a small portion to represent the hundreds.

Our Leaders over the years. Think of Roy Grosbach, Ann Petzel, Josh Doneff, Jen Petzel, Peter Jeans, Justin Lucas, Melissa Dahlman-Babers, Steven Smith, Ian McQueen, Barbie Garnett, Paul Hedin, Hannah and Adam Jensen, Scott and

Stephanie Coultas, and Jerry Nichols as representative of a hundred who have gone into the lives of thousands of kids since 2008.

Young Life kids, like Touya, Chris, Carli, Mallory, Paula, and literally thousands more.

I wish to honor our two Area Directors, Andy Morman and Kaylan Riley. Servants to the core.

Jeff Berget for getting us rolling.

Our IMYL community Volunteers, like Ben and Judy McComb, Mark and Cheryl Footer, Pat Hobin, Laura and Dave Sapienza, Mark and Annemarie Sunderhuse, Tom and Heather Smith, Art and Marcee Martin, Andrew and Katie Smith, Todd and Dawn Andres, Bill and Eunice Senyard, Al and Laura Frei, Jessica Petzel, Brent and Beth Murphy, Blair and Kristina Eklund, Chris and Julie Sharber, Tara and Chet Swint, Ken and Eileen Sloan, Cheryl Holmberg, Jonathan Coors, Fritz and Monica Kerr, Kent and Beth Lepard, John Bellatti, Sean and Sharon Wood, Darrel and Celeste Jones, Michelle and Jeff Spadafora, John Klitzke, Pam and Rob Montgomery, Beverly and Jeffrey Sprout, Ray Zoeller, Dan and Moni McCoy, Kerry and Megan Hicks, Dave and Jill Sneed, Doug and Claudia Downey, Richard and Melanie Crane, Carole and Len Urbas, Carl and Trischa Canter, and Chris and Tyra Kilcullen.

The Mount Evans Qualifying House (The Q House): Troy Erickson, Robyn Hainline, Nancy Taylor, and the five hundred to one thousand boys in juvenile detention I got to know in my ten years as a Leader.

Izale and Jaleesa Williams—and their mom, Margo Williams, who showed me how to cope with difficulties greater than I have ever faced.

My high school Young Life Leader in Omaha, Paul Petersen. Paul, thank you for loving me and showing Christ in you to me.

Ken Tankersley, Kimberly Silvernale, Gill Richard and

Blake Raney, who have tirelessly carried the possibilities and encouragement of YL Committee across the country.

People like TJ Dickerson, Terry Leprino, Zach Kreeger, Jeff Huber, Don Stuber, Skip and Laurie Olson, Cindy Yohann and Brent Cunningham for listening with open minds and merciful hearts.

Thanks to Jeb Baum, Jim Petzel, and Krista and Chad Wallace as IMYL Committee Chairs.

To Ben and Judy McComb, Howard and Ann Hargrove, carriers of the YL torch years before any of us thought about it in Evergreen, Idaho Springs, Baily, Pine, and Conifer.

Young Life Staff including Jacque Abadie, Eric Scofield, Ed Ross, Eugene Luning, Kelsey Jenny, Greg Hook, and Cindy Yohann who unselfishly helped us worship, grieve, think, sing, and laugh.

Our local pastors. Our pastors in our town leading our churches. Adam, John, Philip, Bill, Vera, Lee, Jeff, Jesse, Jason, Josh, and so many more.

Our youth pastors.

Our Bible study leaders.

Our MT 9:38 harvesting workers like Sharon Regan Williams, Nancy Protzman, and Mary Baum.

Our inspirations like Bob and Claudia Mitchell and Newt and Susan Crenshaw.

Special thanks to my brother and friend Ken Tankersley who is an endless inspiration to me.

Special thanks to Claudia Mitchell for her hours, days, meals, and weeks sharing her firsthand experiences for this book.

Special thanks to Andy and Genna Morman and Grace, Ransom, Eden, David, and Cindy Morman.

And my heartfelt thanks to our town, our kids, and to Jesus, our Savior, who—if we are humble enough to submit—is the Lord of our lives.

Printed in the USA
CPSIA information can be obtained
at www.ICGtesting.com
CBHW021335070124
3193CB00004B/13